DON'T LEAVE, PLEASE GO

DON'T LEAVE, PLEASE GO

WHAT YOU (AND YOUR TEEN) NEED TO KNOW BEFORE HEADING TO UNIVERSITY OR COLLEGE

SARA DIMERMAN

PRAISE FOR *DON'T LEAVE, PLEASE GO*

"Sara Dimerman uses her expertise both as a psychologist and mother in such a powerful way. She offers a deeply candid and courageous month-by-month account of her experience with her own daughter in her first year of university. Her book transcends the limitations of a typical advice book, and offers, instead, a guided road map for a healthier transition. It should definitely be on the top of every Grade 12 student's family reading list. When the film's made, I think Meryl Streep should play the mom, Brie Larson the daughter, and Stan Tucci could be a Grade 12 English Creative Writing teacher!"

Domenico Capilongo, High School English Teacher/Teacher Librarian & Dad

"Sara Dimerman takes readers with her on a very personal journey as she journals her way through her daughter's often bumpy, but very relatable, first year away at university. Sara has packed this book with helpful advice for all. With time-synched pointers about what to expect from the final months of Grade 12 to dorm drop-off, through packing up again for summer break, this book reminded me of the wildly popular *What to Expect When You're Expecting*...series for first-time parents—only it's now 18 years later and university-style. A funny, sage and inspirational must-read!"

Janyce Lastman, Education Consultant and Case Manager:
The Tutor Group – and proud Mom of a university graduate

PRAISE FOR *DON'T LEAVE, PLEASE GO*

"*Don't Leave, Please Go* is the essential how-to guide for parents who are torn between being happy that their kids are becoming independent young adults, and being sad that their babies are leaving them. Sara Dimerman helps to navigate the rough terrain in between with kindness, patience and tough love, when necessary. Prepare to have some laughs and shed some tears along the way!"

Barb DiGiulio, Host - The Nightside – Newstalk 1010 Radio & Mom

"As the parent of a teen about to head off to university, I found this book to be a helpful resource. The emotional roller-coaster that both Sara Dimerman and her daughter experienced felt real and allowed me to consider aspects of college life that I otherwise may not have considered. From the transitions between home and school, to the academic demands on the children, and the emotional toll that the social aspect of residence can present, I feel much more prepared for the potential challenges that await. I shared and discussed several sections with my son, and he read the ending that Chloe wrote and he found her words insightful. We also really appreciated the packing list that was included in the appendix. That will absolutely come in handy. I will definitely recommend this book to my friends who are at the same stage of parenting as I am."

Maxelle Yablon, Educator & Mom

Text copyright © 2019 Sara Dimerman

Publishing Assistance and Consulting by:

Publisher Production Solutions

www.publisher-ps.com

Cover Design: 2019 © Talia Dimerman

Book Design: 2019 © Doris Chung

ISBN (softcover): 978-1-9990545-0-2

ISBN (eBook): 978-1-9990545-1-9

Printed in Canada

Dedicated to Chloe Dimerman

For inspiring me and making this book possible

And inspiring others with your insights and contribution

CONTENTS

SECTION FOUR

INTRODUCTION

Attending college or university is not an automatic stepping stone beyond high school for teens in every family. Perhaps your teen is the first in your family to attend a post-secondary institute, perhaps he is following in your footsteps by attending your alma mater or she is carving a path all her own.

For some, it's the program that determines their first choice. For others, it's the prestige of attending a highly-ranked college or university. Some parents proudly wear shirts with the name of the institution across their chests or affix magnets and bumper stickers to their cars.

Regardless of where your teen is going or why, the process of applying, being accepted or denied and the emotions that go along with this, are similar for everyone.

For teens who are staying at home and commuting to university or college, there will be lots of changes (such as commuting distance daily, meeting new people and sitting in lecture halls as opposed to classrooms, for example). I remember our family adventure about a month before our older daughter, who had never travelled the subway on her own, was to begin her one-hour daily commute to university from the sleepy suburbs to foreign territory downtown. We had planned out the route, including walking from the subway to her academic destination.

To begin, we all rode the same subway car. Then, part way, we exited one train and waited for the next so that she could ride in one car and us in another and she could experience how it felt to be alone. When we reached our stop, we exited and reunited on the platform.

I shall never forget how, as she emerged from her car, so, too, did a man who appeared to be at least 10 years older than her. He began by telling her how photogenic she appeared and asked if she wanted to join him for a photo shoot. I shudder to think how much worse she would have felt had we not been only a few feet away, as she ignored him and dashed in our direction, instead.

She was quite shaken and so were we. In some way, however, it may have gotten some of what she was fearful might happen, out of the way, and prepared her for knowing that despite what or who came her way, she could deal with it. Coming home, despite her experience, she took the train ahead of us, which was a step closer to her travelling solo only a month later.

For those transitioning from home to live in residence, the changes are magnified by living so independently, further apart from friends and family and sleeping in an unfamiliar environment.

Living apart is certainly one factor taken into consideration when sending out applications. Some teens are sure that this is part of the experience they have been looking forward to. Other teens (and parents) consider living apart from one another as part of the financial and emotional price they are willing to pay in exchange for a coveted spot at a sought-out institute. Still, when everything is said and done, and the time to leave draws closer, it's often hard for both parents and teens to imagine that they will go from living under the same roof one day to living hours apart the next.

If you're like most parents and teens, you can put these anxiety-provoking thoughts aside when you're in the planning stage, especially since it feels as though there is a lot of time before the start of that new chapter in your lives.

However, when the acceptance letters arrive and it's time to accept or deny the offers, that's when it becomes more real and sometimes, too close for comfort. Many parents celebrate with more enthusiasm than their teens, others rejoice together and still others, out of fear that their child will not be able to cope living alone when the time comes, may find reasons or excuses as to why their child should not go after all.

Many teens to whom I have spoken say that they feel that when their parents tell them that it's a bad idea or that they should not live away from home, that they are trying to control them. I try to help teens see that what may be perceived as control, may actually be fears being felt by the parent.

As a psychologist, my professional role, often, is to work with these families to understand the consequences of parents standing in the way of a teen who desperately wants that away-from-home experience. Now that I've had the opportunity to experience one child attending university while living at home and another child living several hours away, I can say with confidence that as long as the teen is wanting it as much or more than you, then the living-away experience is to be encouraged and supported.

I recommend not creating roadblocks for your teen, because living away in residence is not just about growing academically, but in so many other ways, too. So, if you as a typical parent, are feeling somewhat anxious or stressed about what's to come, rest assured that you are not alone, but that in facing your fears and letting your child go, you are truly giving him or her a gift!

Part of what kept me going during my younger daughter's first year away in residence at university, was retreating into my head at the end of each day and recording my thoughts and the day's events on my laptop. It was therapeutic journalling at its best. And also, an opportunity to record events that neither she nor I would likely remember as vividly 10 years from now.

She didn't know I was doing this at the time and I didn't tell her, because I didn't want any of our interactions to be contrived or for her to say "I hope you don't write about this tonight". (She's now approved everything I've written about her on these pages.) I knew that ultimately, I wanted to work my writing journal into book form so that I could share our experiences with other parents and their teens. It's helpful to know that what you are going through is normal and expected, and that despite some difficulties along the way, things do get better.

By the end of my daughter's first year at university, I had more than 100,000 words written. By way of comparison, a 200-page book is typically around less than half of that.

So, editing was a big part of what was required to prepare this book. I hope that you—as a parent—find helpful tips and ideas on almost every page. I also hope that you feel less anxious about what is to come after reading it.

Some of what you read may surprise or concern you. It may even make you feel more anxious at first. However, I believe that it's better to be prepared before your teen leaves so that you are not blindsided along the way.

My hope is that you will share some of what you learn with your teen along his or her journey, when or if the time is right, so that they, too, can know that they're not alone. Reading my daughter's reflections at the end of the book will hopefully also inspire and encourage your teen to keep going, even when the going is tough.

SECTION ONE

BEFORE THE BIG MOVE

CHAPTER ONE

SIX WEEKS AND COUNTING!

I walked past my 18-year-old daughter's bedroom tonight as I have a million times before, and saw what I often see—a wet towel on her carpeted floor, tousled clothes on her chair and throw pillows cast to one side. But tonight, instead of asking her to hang up the clothes and towel and to straighten her room, I bit my tongue and reminded myself that we had only weeks to go before loading up the rented truck with paraphernalia we have been acquiring for the past few months, including the mini fridge and mattress topper loaned to us, the new printer, router, and chair she may never sit in at her desk (she typically works from her bed). All I have to endure is another six weeks until I walk past her pristinely made bed, her freshly vacuumed carpeted floor, and everything in its place.

But this knowledge leads to a familiar gnawing in my stomach, because I think I will soon long for her to be home—despite the unmade bed and clothes draped over the chair.

I think I might even miss nagging her to go to bed before midnight, long to hear her in muffled conversation with her boyfriend, long to see her walk through the front door after school at 3:30 p.m. each day.

So, along with the short-lived relief I feel in knowing that I will no longer have to wake as early to make her school lunch (my choice, I know), enjoy not having to go into her room every five minutes to make sure she's awake in time for school (another choice), I am preparing myself for the longer term pain I expect to feel, for the void in our home without her in it.

CHAPTER TWO

HUNTING AND GATHERING

("DO YOU REALLY NEED ANOTHER COLOURED MARKER?")

I was excited to learn about Bed Bath & Beyond's Campus Ready Shopping Events, which allow university and college bound students to get a jump start on their move and take advantage of solutions Bed Bath & Beyond has to offer.

Wanting to miss the crowds, we arrived 10 minutes before our assigned 6 p.m. time slot, and once my daughter's name had been verified on a list, we were handed a very complete and specific list of what she would need for her particular residence—right down to the size of the bed and whether or not she was "allowed" to bring a toaster oven or kettle (she had already decided she was going to anyway).

We were also told about their special Pack & Hold program, which allowed us to shop at our local Bed Bath & Beyond for items she wasn't taking with her that evening, and then pick up and pay for them on or before her move-in day at a Bed Bath & Beyond store closest to her university. A relief not to have to cart even more stuff with us on our three-hour car journey to her new home for the upcoming school year.

It felt completely overwhelming at first. It's hard enough to go shopping for a duvet and sheet set, but add that to dozens of other must haves and it's enough to make anyone's head spin. In addition, because the savvy assistant who was assigned to us, suggested that I could take advantage of the event myself, I didn't want to miss out on the opportunity of selecting items I wanted, too!

I knew since we hadn't yet had dinner (making us relatively hungry) and that my daughter and I might feel and think differently about what she really needed, and how much should be spent on even those things I agreed to, that this evening was ripe for disagreement between us. So, I put on my happy face and made a mental note to have fun, even if the calculator in my head was adding numbers beyond my comfort zone.

I pretended that we had been awarded a shopping spree and that money was no object. An adventure. An occasion we would look back on with fond memories. I was suddenly brought back to reality after she exclaimed how desperately she needed a body pillow and wait for it... decorative throw pillows!

That's when I forgot about the pretense and said, "if you want throw pillows, feel free to take those that will be sitting lonely on your bed at home while you are gone".

Overall, we survived the shopping trip without a fight. Standing in line to check out the few items we wanted to take home that evening, I saw that we were not alone. Parents and their teens were engaged in similar conversations and debates over wants versus needs, while other peers stood in the long lineup to cash out; comparing their choice of colour combinations. "I'm going with mostly grey and white," I heard one say to another "with a splash of yellow because I figure it would look too boring without it."

Once the bigger items had been either purchased or chosen, my daughter showed me a very comprehensive list she had prepared of smaller must haves. Truth be told, I was impressed and excited. Impressed at how thorough her hand-written list was—with hand-drawn blocks next to each, waiting for a check mark as she worked towards making sure she wasn't forgetting anything. I was excited that she had seen the method in my list-making madness. Not only had she decided to transfer the digital list she had created on her phone, but she had gone a step further to make sure that everything was accounted for.

She even allowed me to share my list (of course I had one—I'd been creating it for months) with her just in case I might have a few items she hadn't already thought of. There was, to my delight, very little I had to offer.

With list in hand, we went to the dollar store in search of items not yet ticked off. I gave her credit for reminding me that many of the dollar store items were the same that we would be paying triple for at the local grocery store. Again, wanting this to be a memorable experience between us and knowing that no matter how hard we tried, the cost would be nominal compared to the items purchased earlier, I followed her lead up and down the aisles.

We stopped at the cleaning supplies section and debated the pros and cons of a hand-held sponge for washing dishes (even though she also insisted on buying paper plates just in case she wasn't in the mood to cart her plastic plates to the sink) versus one with a handle, which I tried to convince her might not do as good a job. Ultimately, she chose what she wanted and I figured this was something I could certainly allow her to learn about on her own.

I bit my tongue when she placed the red solo drinking cups and ping pong balls into the cart and then added the matching shot cups. Better that she buys drinking game items in my presence, I reminded myself. She considered and then put back the glue gun, the markers and pens and pencils (I pleaded with her to go through several drawers at home to sort them out first before she bought more—even reminded her about the landfill sites being so overloaded—and she didn't put up a fuss).

She added the dart board because its colours matched that of her university (how could I say no?), the wine glasses, the extra-large water bottle, the jars that had 'utensils' and 'tea' written on the front in bold letters, a peeler and a pair of scissors (she had to start fresh with a new one after all) and many other items that I'm sure would bore you if I listed them all (but I have anyway in Appendix A at the end of the book).

The cashier didn't seem too impressed as we unloaded all the items on the counter in front of her. She had to call for backup and seemed quite put out when I asked if she could put the two small bottles of dishwashing liquid into a separate bag in case they leaked. After all was said and done, we walked out with $128.01 worth of products, which wasn't too expensive considering all that we bought.

CHAPTER THREE

PRACTICAL PREPAREDNESS 101

("HOW WILL YOU GET YOURSELF UP IN THE MORNING WITHOUT MY HELP?")

Trying to prepare your child to live in residence and be away from home for the first time can feel overwhelming. When you're used to being able to get to their school in a very short period of time, when needed, being called to their bed at midnight when they're not feeling well or to get rid of the spider that's crawling on the ceiling above their head, it's difficult for parents, and sometimes teens, to think about not living in close proximity.

In addition, if they're not used to taking care of themselves because you've considered it your responsibility and pleasure to always pack their school lunch, to make sure that they are up in time for school and that their laundry is washed and neatly folded, there's good reason to think that they might not be ready for what lies ahead.

The tricky part is getting them on board before they leave, because the last thing most teens want is to shadow you when you're doing laundry or preparing their food, so that they can learn how. What we take for granted as being simple tasks because we've become so good at them over the years, might appear as complex mathematical equations to them. So, not only are they not interested in wrapping their heads around these chores, because they seem too tedious or difficult, but also because they typically don't think as far into the future as we do. They believe that they will just figure it out when they need to. And you know what? They may be right, because if you're not around to show them, then they can just watch a YouTube video, Google the information or chat with you online so that you can coach as they do whatever it is.

However, I did try.

Monday is laundry day in our home. I tried to get my daughter on board to join me in the laundry room in the basement more than once. Now that there are only two Mondays left before she leaves us, I have very little time left to teach the ins and outs of laundry 101. The pressure is on!

She wasn't a willing participant, but at some point, she asked: "Can I put all my clothes in the washing machine together?" At first, my answer was a resounding no. Honestly, you want to take all the clothes I have meticulously cared for over the years, throw them all into the (probably old) washing machine and hope for the best? I am fully aware that her clothes will likely not look the same as when she takes them away from the only closet they have ever known; that sorting, separating, choosing the correct temperature on the washer and hanging them to dry will not be her priority at university, nor should be, but I wanted to make the best of a potentially bad situation.

Another time she asked: "Should I take slippers with me?" Just when I thought that we couldn't possibly have left anything off the list we had collaborated on (we even have 'AquaFlops' shower shoes from Bed Bath & Beyond, designed with holes in them to let the water seep through), she was asking about slippers.

Slippers in residence are probably a good idea. Who knows what her floor will be covered with? Tiles? Carpet? Regardless, slippers make sense. "Yes, I think slippers are a great idea, good thinking!" I responded, grateful that she was asking for my opinion, but also thinking for herself.

"How will I get myself up in the morning?" is another common question, and worry, of a teen moving away from home.

One of the most aggravating things I find as a parent is waking my children up—often several times and despite an alarm beeping—in the morning so that they won't be late for class or work. I do this despite philosophically believing that they should be responsible for getting themselves out of bed in time and for experiencing the consequences if they don't.

I have threatened not to wake them up at times, and have even managed to delay getting them up (so that they are somewhat late, but not terribly), but I have never managed to walk away without making them aware that they have slept beyond the time they had hoped to wake.

So, it's no surprise for me to hear my daughter's concern about getting herself up in time for class. Yes, I could become her human alarm clock when she's away, but deep down I know that would not do her much good.

Besides, I run the risk of becoming panic stricken every time I try to reach her, only to hear her voice mail message.

My thinking is that, like most people, my daughter will find a way to get herself up on time in the morning when she knows that she only has herself to rely on. In the meantime, instead of giving her the answer to this concern, I helped her brainstorm possible solutions, of which there were several. So, she may set a series of alarm reminders over five-minute intervals in order to make sure she's successful (because she often wakes briefly, turns off the alarm and goes back to sleep), or she may try something else, but I feel confident she will manage this one.

Another common teen concern is: "How will I manage homework assignments without reminders and help?"

As parents, we often feel that it is our responsibility to ensure that our children are responsible and punctual. While that is indeed part of what we hope to instill when parenting, there comes a time when they need to deal with the consequences of their own behaviour. Unfortunately, if we continue to stand over, supervise and nag them, they will be less equipped to manage themselves when they leave high school to live on their own.

When my daughter was in Grade 12 (and even in Grade 11), it was quite liberating when I came to realize that since she was so close to living independently, that I should hand her the reins and let her be the driver when it came to managing her academic responsibilities, which included attendance.

There are so many other practical issues that will be raised by both you and your teen before and during their time away. Try to remain patient and collaborate on solutions as much as possible, as you both prepare for your teen's typically much greater independence and autonomy than ever before.

CHAPTER FOUR

SAYING GOODBYE TO FAMILY AND FRIENDS

SO LONG TO SIBLINGS

Our oldest daughter was eight years old when our second was born. We didn't plan on having such a big gap between them, but nature interfered with our plan and two miscarriages later, our much-wanted baby was born. Talia was thrilled about becoming a big sister and was old enough to enjoy the pregnancy and anticipation of a new baby in the family with us. In fact, she even helped us come up with her sister's name, Chloe.

An eight-year age gap allowed us to parent as if we had two only children. There was no jealousy when our second was born, because our older child understood why we had to take care of a baby as we did and besides, she was already actively involved in her drama and dance classes and spending time with her friends when she wasn't at school.

When she was home, she was more than happy to share the limelight with her sister and to show her how to hold a crayon, to feed herself or to dance and sing to Spice Girls songs. She was happy to play big sister and to see her baby sister in her hand-me-down dresses and to paint her nails or braid her hair.

However, as time marched on, and as our younger daughter became more independent, and not as much in need of her sister's attention, their relationship changed. Our younger daughter wanted to prove herself as being self-reliant and by doing so, rebelled against and even shirked some of her sister's influence.

As much as many parents want their children to love each other unconditionally and to be there for each other now and "when we are gone," I know that in reality, this doesn't always happen. Often, siblings get along better when they are living apart and away from family dynamics.

And for siblings who are close, saying goodbye or coming to terms with one moving away from home, can be very difficult. If you have children who are mostly well connected and enjoy spending time with one another, don't be surprised if perhaps as a way of dealing with the impending separation, that their relationship shifts. They may become less patient with one another, quicker to anger or have disagreements more often.

Our older daughter made mention that she couldn't wait to be our "only child" again. And our younger daughter has made mention of the same (since daughter number one has plans to move out herself soon). As the oldest of four siblings, I can't say I blame them. It's sometimes wonderful to have a sibling, or more, but it's also nice to have your parent's full attention.

FAREWELL TO FAMILY

Not only is there a shift in dynamics between siblings as the departure date looms, but between teens and their parents, too. There's a feeling in the air that is somewhat unsettling. Family members are more easily triggered by one another. Feelings more easily hurt.

One night, after an altercation between my younger daughter and me, I left her room in a huff after saying something in regards to being upset that we weren't spending more quality time together before she left. As I descended the stairs, I heard her call out, "You better get used to it. You won't be able to come into my room and just hang out with me in a few weeks".

Of course, I knew that. I think that she (even if not on as conscious a level) knew it, too, and that she was trying increased separation on for size.

A friend of mine, living in the USA, said that as the day came closer for her daughter to leave for university about an hour's drive away, she became more "testy" and challenging to live with. My friend said that she was actually counting down the days in anticipation of them taking a break from one another and that she was ready for her daughter to fly the coop. This is not uncommon, as both parents and their teens begin the natural process of separation from one another.

I ordered her favorite caramel crunch cake with a 'good luck' inscription on it to serve at our extended family farewell get-together and purchased a large body pillow (yes, I gave in to her wanting one) that had the inscription 'Be your best beautiful you' on it. I also managed to figure out how to use the photo printing kiosk at a local retail outlet so that I could print 10 photos that I've taken over the past few weeks of her friends and us so that she had photographic reminders of what she would come home to.

"I think I may be lonely in residence," she shared with her cousin at the get-together.

"But why would you be lonely?" her cousin asked, "there are so many people on the floor with you."

"But it's still different to being at home," she said.

Later she confessed that even though she enjoys being on her own in her room at home, it's comforting just knowing that we are in the house with her.

FAREWELL TO OLD FRIENDS

I believe it is just luck of the draw as to whether or not kids connect to other kids in their classroom. It starts in Kindergarten and then, depending on how divided they are through Grades 1 and 8 especially (since in most cities in Canada they begin high school in Grade 9 and may be in different classrooms to one another), they either stay gelled or not.

My daughter was very lucky to have been placed with and be part of a great group of kids (and in turn, we were introduced to a great group of parents), right from the start. There were about a dozen kids that were constantly in each other's midst (give or take a few more or less depending on the year and what was going on in their lives) both at school and outside of school, especially in the lower grades.

When they went to high school, they kept their friendships alive, either in the same elective or mandatory subject, or after school when socializing. As is normal, along the way, there were politics and parting of ways between some and even reconciliations. Grades 11 and 12 were more disconnecting years for many of the kids, as they evolved into young adults, formed relationships with significant others (and sometimes had to find a balance, as our daughter did when she found a steady boyfriend at the age of 16).

After all of their post-secondary school paths were chosen (most are moving away from home for university or college, some are staying at home and commuting and a few are going for a victory lap), and after their graduation ceremony and party, it seemed that most of the original peer group started to come together again.

With increased urgency they are going out and spending time chillin' at each other's homes until the early hours of the morning (and sometimes even all crashing at someone's house). With increased fervency they are clinging to one another. One of our daughter's closest friends is going to university a plane ride away. Because of the distance, I think that saying goodbye to this friend is hitting my daughter the hardest and they're already planning a reunion at the first opportunity.

I see that our daughter is sharing in our experience of loss and excitement.

Hopefully, between peers, the emotions are reciprocated and shared. Perhaps tears are even shed.

The night before the first of her longtime school friends, Madison, was leaving with her mom, Andrea, on their two-day driving adventure (along with their two 80-pound dogs) to Halifax, the city in which she was going to be living and studying, we arranged for a group of us to meet at a local coffee shop. My daughter gave Madison a goodbye letter and made her swear that she wouldn't open it until they were well on their way.

After an hour and a bit together, drinking café lattes, hot chocolate and talking about how our lives were changing, the "kids" began texting other friends for an impromptu meet-up at their elementary school to take a picture of the group in the same spot that they had all assembled prior to graduating from Grade 8.

It was raining lightly when we arrived. The area was pitch black, except for the headlights from the parents' cars as they waited for the rest of the group to arrive. As self-appointed official photographer, I stood in the rain and watched as eight of the original 12 friends came together. Hysterical with laughter, they tried to fit as they once did, in the circular cut-out of the wall in front of the school's front doors. Four years later they had grown quite a bit and fitting comfortably wasn't so easy, but as snug as they were, they managed to pose for a series of pictures.

As I watched and took photographs, a wave of nostalgia washed over me. How quickly time had flown. From little giggling girls with pigtails and little boys with high pitched voices and baseball caps, they had grown into mature young women and men, all standing at the threshold of the rest of their lives, but still holding onto every last precious moment together. The rain fell gently, falling on my cheeks and mixing with salty tears.

CHAPTER FIVE

TOO CLOSE FOR COMFORT?

Two weeks today, my daughter will be entering into Frosh Week. A week of getting to know her fellow student residents and perhaps a roommate (she doesn't find out the details of her living arrangements in residence for another week). Like most teens headed away from home very soon, my daughter admits to feeling "scared about living on my own and having to do everything myself like laundry, cleaning and organizing my own schedule". On the other hand, she is also "looking forward to living on my own and not having anyone telling me what to do".

We will be moving her in over the first long weekend in September and have decided to drive to the university (in a borrowed truck because we didn't book a U-Haul with enough time to secure one) the day before move in, have a restful (maybe) night's sleep at a hotel nearby and then after moving her in, to sleep over another night before driving back home. Even though the drive is only about three hours each way, I figure we're going to need the respite after the commotion of move-in day, despite my daughter not being happy about this. I'm thinking that, although she would never admit to this, saying goodbye to us will be a little like the first day of Kindergarten. Although she is grown now and so much more independent and self-assured, separation may be a little bit more difficult for her than she would ever let on—even to herself.

Just as Kindergarten teachers often recommend that parents not tarry after dropping their kids off, because just the sight of us can make emotions surge, so, too, might our stay overnight create more separation anxiety and prolong the adjustment of her being comfortable alone. Despite recognizing this, and of course not wanting her to suffer for even a second more than she needs to, I think we will need a chance to catch our breath (and to have a "good" cry) before returning to a home without her in it every day.

I also believe that there is a practical component to staying an extra day. Who knows what extra little item she will need (despite all that we have already bought) that we can pick up for her the day after move in? So, I tell myself that if she has to wait one extra day to start the process of adjustment, that's not such a bad thing. Besides, as parents, don't we have to think of what's good for us, too—just some of the time?

I met one of my closest friends, Christine, at the fitness club. While working out together, she reminded me that she has only 10 days left before they drive her only son (she has a younger daughter, too) to university about an hour away. "I walked past his bedroom this morning and saw those two big feet sticking out from under his covers and was glad to see him exactly where he belongs. I know I should be happy that he's following his passion, but I can't help but feel a gnawing sadness inside of me. I think I'm experiencing the feelings I associate with profound loss."

Later that day as my daughter stood at the kitchen sink, washing her lunch plate, I could tell that she appeared sad. I stood beside her and gently placed my hand on her back, not knowing how she would respond to my touch. I was relieved that she felt able to turn towards me, allowed me to hold her as she placed her head on my shoulder and showed vulnerability as she let her tears flow for a few minutes, as she experienced this loss and change in her life, too.

I reminded her of how normal it was to be experiencing a bunch of different emotions as she stood on the precipice of the next chapter of her life, without most familiar friends and family by her side.

When she pulled back, I saw that she appeared less sad. Perhaps as a result of knowing that what she was feeling was entirely normal…was entirely OK.

We spent the rest of the day inching closer to her leaving home. In two weeks from now she will have been at her residence for four days. Four days into her four-year post-secondary commitment.

For the remainder of the week I was in the 'nesting' phase, just as when I was pregnant. You may remember what you were doing just weeks prior to your baby being born. I remember myself underneath the dining room table, polishing the legs with wood polish and overturning drawers, throwing things out and organizing the rest. This all in order to prepare ourselves for the arrival of our newborn. Now, too, is a period of rebirth. As our family prepares for this new phase of life, my daughter and I are going through clothing closets, organizing drawers, clearing clutter and anticipating the day that she moves away.

One day, she reluctantly followed me into the basement where I kept an extra-large plastic bin of scraps and memorabilia I had collected throughout her life—random notes she had written to me—"you're the menist mom" and "I love you very much" at different stages of life. Get well notes to her after her tonsillectomy so many years ago, certificates of achievement, letters from the tooth fairy (written by her older sister), and of course a birth announcement and clippings from the newspaper on the day she was born.

Although I had wanted her to go through everything with me, as it turned out, going through the scrap box was more for me than her. I realized that this is all part of my preparation for the day that my "baby" is leaving and that getting all of the "scraps" in order is not only my way of organizing her life with me until this point in time, but also how I am coping with my soaring separation anxiety.

The next day, we spent a few hours at the mall, trying to find clothing items she needed after filling three big bags of clothing from her closet to either give away because they no longer fit, wouldn't be worn ever again or to be sold on some online site.

As we went from store to store, I exercised patience that even I didn't know existed. I bit my tongue when she took an item off the rack, allowing her to figure out why it wasn't going to be what she looked best in. I also refrained from saying anything when she said, "I need to find some party items. You know I'm going to be partying a lot".

What I felt like saying was "are you kidding? Don't you know what can happen if you party too much?"

Instead, I reminded myself how lucky I am to have a daughter who so comfortably and casually remarks about her intentions. "Maybe I need something leather?" she asked. I moved to the other rack, pretending not to have heard.

She followed me and pulled a t-shirt off the rack, asking if I wanted to try it on. Across the front was written: 'warrior, not worrier'. So apt, I thought. Yes, my goal is to be a warrior, not a worrier, while she is away and I think she plans on being one, too—even though we both know that it's normal to feel some anxiety along the way.

At the end of the day, as is my routine most nights before getting into bed myself, I check in with my daughters in their bedrooms—directly across from one another. Part of the ritual is to sit on their beds to chat for as long as they will allow me to. Sometimes, it's to remind them of the time (although I'm sure they're aware but not concerned about it) and to suggest that they turn off their lights. I realize that as young adults and on the verge of taking care of themselves completely, I shouldn't be reminding them to turn off their lights, but still do because I can't help but believe that my husband and I suffer the next day when they're cranky and difficult to talk to.

Most nights, despite my best efforts, I turn off my light while theirs are still on. Just as I did last night, when I heard my younger daughter call out, "Mom?" Ah, the sweetness of hearing the word only they get to use. "Yes?" I responded questioningly, knowing that "mom?" is typically a prelude to "can you get me some water?" or, "can you get me something off the printer tomorrow morning?" She continued, "can you come here, please?" She has asked this before and I jump to attention, because this often means that she wants to talk in the safety of the dark. We've had some of our best conversations in her bed after the lights are turned off.

When she was much younger, I sometimes thought of this as being manipulative—to allow her more time awake. But as she got older, I think it was more about not having to look me in the eyes, something about allowing herself to be vulnerable and to expose her feelings through her words and nothing else. So, even when I am dead tired and looking forward to closing my eyes until the morning, I dare not miss the opportunity to connect with my child.

"Yes?" I said, standing at her doorway. "Can you tickle my back?" she asked in a soft voice. How could I resist? Even though my hand was heavy with tiredness and it was difficult to keep awake in the quiet of the dark room, I contoured my body next to hers in her twin-sized bed. I breathed in the coconut smell of her recently shampooed hair, I tickled her back and massaged her head as she requested. Oh, how blessed I felt. She thought that she was the one being soothed, but I felt it, too. As I lay there, tears sprung to my eyes and I was glad she could not see them, because I didn't want this to be a sad moment or one in which she would feel a need to comfort me. All the while, I soaked in what might be one of the last times in a long time that she would ask me to snuggle with her. For now, being with her allowed me, for a brief moment in time, to recapture a special connection and to hold onto that nostalgically—especially when, in a couple of weeks, I will only have one "child" to nag at midnight.

My husband and I spent a weekend away in Montreal to celebrate the marriage of our friends' son and his bride. At this stage of our lives, we no longer talk to other similar aged parents about toilet training or temper tantrums. Most of the couples we meet have children who are attending or have graduated university or college, some are even married and have children of their own.

Corrina, another guest at the wedding, shared how she and her husband of 30 years, after raising their children in Winnipeg, followed them both to Montreal where they were studying at McGill University. After graduation, however, one daughter found work in Toronto and the other worked in New York.

Corrina told me that she and her husband, Martin, now find themselves thinking about where they want to continue their retirement—in Montreal (in between their two children) or in the city where one of them lives. Despite being young retirees, still very compatible and enjoying their time as a couple, she talked about how she cries every time she has to say goodbye to either one of their daughters. "I thought it would have gotten easier by now" she shared with me, "but I guess I'm not that strong."

"Strong?" I questioned. "I don't see that as being a sign of weakness, but more a sign of loving. How can you not cry when you're leaving a part of your heart with them?"

"How are you feeling about Chloe leaving for university?" I asked my husband on the train ride from Montreal back to Toronto. I suspected that he might be having similar feelings to me, but dads (even those who are comfortable sharing emotion, as my husband is) tend not to talk about their feelings regarding being separated from their kids as much as moms do. I learned that my husband's feelings echo mine, but he is more of a realist. "It's about the passage of time," he said. "Seeing our children grow up and go off on their own reminds us of how much time has passed. And it's what's supposed to happen." There, with the clickety clack of the train on the track, as we, too, continued on our passage, we talked some more about the pros and cons of having our children leave the nest. On one hand, eternally grateful that they are healthy and capable enough to do so, and a little bit relieved not to worry about what we will make for dinner every night (daughter number two hates leftovers), or dealing with the arguments between our daughters, but also feeling a pulling at our heartstrings that our family of four will be changing forevermore.

With only a week to go, it's crunch time. Seems that no matter how many months we've planned for this and no matter how many lists we've created, there are always last-minute items to add. Small items such as needle and thread, Polysporin, After Bite, nail scissors and a thermometer (my daughter asked for this). You'd think that she was going to some remote island in the middle of the Atlantic Ocean with no access to a drug store. But these are not entirely rational decisions. They are emotional. The moments during which moms, especially, want to make sure that their children have everything they need.

With only a few days to go, we went through my daughter's shoes. I held each pair towards her and asked, "leave, give away or take with?" By the time she had assigned at least 10 pairs of shoes, three pairs of boots and two pairs of sandals to the 'take with' pile, I panicked at the thought of not only having to make room for them in the truck we rented (it's beginning to feel more like we should have hired a moving company!) but that she was not going to have space in her room for anything other than shoes.

But try as I might to help her see this through my lens, she was dead set against leaving anything behind and since I am trying to keep peace over our last few days together, I let it go. Hey, I guess the worst that can happen is that she has to eliminate a few items when the truck is fully loaded or that we bring half a truck full of items back home with us because she's run out of space in her room.

With only a day to go before leaving, I was asked to be a guest on a radio talk show. The host wanted to chat about back to school jitters—especially because he was anticipating taking his almost four-year-old son to Junior Kindergarten and wanted to make sure that he wasn't alone in feeling as he did. He shared that he and his wife had already planned on drowning their sorrows over pancakes after dropping him off. I reminded him (and myself) that along with the tears, that he and his wife might also want to consider how wonderful it is that their son is able to attend school and that they are all able to take part in one of life's milestones.

I knew that the remainder of the day would be a hectic one. It reminded me of how I feel on the day before leaving on a big trip. There were lists on every level of the house and boxes that appeared to be multiplying by the hour. There were also heightened emotions all round. Eventually I calmed down, trusting that everything was in order…until I saw the mound of clothing on my daughter's bed (about three quarters of what had previously hung in her closet) that she was yet to pack. I panicked. I hadn't yet seen the rental truck (which my husband said was a "beast" after picking it up), but still, I wondered how much even a beast could hold.

Together we worked on packing one large suitcase and a duffel bag. She suggested rolling, instead of folding the clothes, to save room in the duffel bag and I tried to help by letting her know that they still needed to be folded before being rolled unless she wanted them to be completely creased when she took them out of the bag. I suggested she take an iron, but she said she would not use it. She said she would just pull the material into shape if it was too creased, but I suggested putting it into the dryer for 10 minutes instead.

"Are you kidding," she said, "why would I do that? It costs money to use the dryer, you know."

I hoped that all her clothes wouldn't look like she'd slept in them (oh well, I guess there are worse things, I thought, and remembered to ask myself "who owns this problem anyway?").

By the time we were all packed, my husband returned home with the beast and yes, with the last row of seats down, it looked like it would hold a lot. Nevertheless, a fridge, a fan, and many boxes later, there wasn't a square inch of space left. We did manage to squeeze an umbrella in, though, just in case. We had debated packing the beast a day later, but in hindsight I'm glad that we packed that day. One less stressor for when we leave.

Upon surveying the house and her bedroom after everything was packed, my daughter realized that there were quite a few items that had been forgotten—a flat iron for her hair, headphones to listen to music, some more toiletries and games, to name but a few, so we had to resort to packing another small suitcase to hold the almost forgotten items. It reminded me of when you've sold your home and the movers have taken most of the items, as you find this and that forgotten item. Upon checking my list, I realized that I hadn't yet brought up the long-handled floor mop with the micro-fibre pad to clean her floor upon arrival.

"You're not taking that, are you?" my daughter asked with a horrified look on her face, as I brought it upstairs.

"Why the look?" I asked.

"Well, firstly because we can't fit it in the truck and secondly because I will never use it," she scolded.

"What will you use to clean your floor?" I asked.

"I have a mini vacuum," she responded.

"But that isn't enough," I replied. "You mean to tell me that you're going to live in a room for an entire school year and never mop the floor?"

"You got it!" she responded in a smart alecky way.

Then I snapped. Under the weight of a stressful series of days, I had reached my breaking point.

"You sound so ungrateful," I snarled. "Why can't you just thank me for helping you?"

Well, actually what I really said was, "you're acting like an ungrateful brat". I wasn't proud of my outburst, but it was too late. She looked upset, but she must have realized some truth in what I was saying, because she didn't respond.

Later, as she was getting ready to go out for her last evening in a while with old friends, I came into her room to ask if she wanted to have dinner with us.

"You didn't knock," she admonished, likely still not feeling too warm and fuzzy following our earlier exchange.

It's true. I hadn't, but give me a break—it had been a long day. I turned around quickly and retreated to my room and my keyboard to begin recording our last day before she leaves. About 10 minutes later she strode into my room.

"You didn't knock," I said. I couldn't resist.

She handed me an envelope.

She's giving her notice, I thought, but I said nothing.

On the outside she had written "Mom and Dad" with a heart around the words.

"Don't read it without dad," she said.

I felt a lump in my throat.

"Will I cry?" I asked.

"Maybe," she said.

And then she was gone out to dinner with a quick goodbye.

I sat next to my husband on the couch and opened the envelope. It read: "Dear mom and dad"…and then she went on to share how she had been reflecting on how she got from being a little girl in her pink and purple room playing with Barbies, to where she is today. She gave us mounds of credit for helping her grow into the person she feels she is—confident and capable of making good decisions and knowing right from wrong, capable of making lists (yay, I will take credit for that) and cooking a few dishes (my husband is the mastermind behind that).

She asked us to trust in her ability to continue to grow and fly and that we should feel good in knowing that we had prepared her well for where she is now.

She wrote about being "terrified" by what she was about to embark upon, about stepping out of her comfort zone, but feeling the importance of doing it anyway.

She wrote about how she knows that we want to hold onto her (and then that she wants to hold onto us, too, which felt good, but kind of hard to read), and that she understood how we must be feeling. She ended by writing how much she loves us.

By the end of the letter, of course my husband and I were both in tears.

SECTION TWO

THE BIG MOVE

CHAPTER SIX

THE JOURNEY BEGINS

Even though she wasn't scheduled to move into her assigned single-person room until the following day, our plan was to arrive in time to pick up the items we had ordered from Bed Bath & Beyond, some grocery items (we called ahead to the hotel to make sure that there was a fridge in the room) and then to meet my daughter's elementary school friend and her family with whom we have maintained a relationship since the kids were in Kindergarten together, for supper. Luckily, we called well ahead to make a reservation, because many of the restaurants had been booked up for weeks prior to this busy move-in weekend.

We knew that once we had picked up our Pack & Hold at Bed Bath & Beyond, there wouldn't be a square inch of space in the vehicle to accommodate our daughters, so we dropped them off at the hotel (some have special rates for students' families, by the way). This allowed them to drop their small bags off, and then go shopping and exploring the town together, and we went off to do the not as much fun stuff.

As we anticipated, getting everything in, even without passengers, was a squeeze, but somehow, we managed with barely enough space to accommodate a few bags of essentials, such as milk, bread, peanut butter, yoghurt, baby carrots and some fruit, from the grocery store.

At dinner, my daughter and her friend talked excitedly (and nervously) about the big move in the following morning. Unfortunately, since their residence and type of room accommodation was mostly luck of the draw, (although some students do get letters from professionals requesting specific forms of accommodation for one reason or another) they were living in different residences about 10 minutes walk away from each other. In addition, her friend's move in was for 8 a.m. and my daughter's was at noon. At her university, the time depended on whether you had been placed on an odd or even floor.

After a short walk through town after dinner, our friends went back to the hotel in preparation for their early morning wake up and we headed over to Chloe's boyfriend's home, which he is renting with three of his first-year buddies (he is going into his second year at the same university). He's so happy about not having to share a shower and sink with so many residence floormates and not having to eat cafeteria food ever again.

Lying in bed at the hotel that night, I reflected on the day that was. Knowing what the next day would bring, I must confess I was feeling particularly vulnerable, anticipating saying goodbye with a great deal of trepidation and concern about how it was going to impact all of us.

CHAPTER SEVEN

MOVE-IN DAY
WHAT TO EXPECT

Since the four of us were sharing one hotel room, I noticed that my daughter had a difficult time getting out of bed today. No one spoke much. I was tiptoeing on eggshells, afraid of saying the wrong thing. Later, over breakfast, I made the mistake of asking how she was feeling (how could a psychologist mom not?) and she jumped down my throat with "do you really have to ask me that? I don't want to talk about it". I retreated quickly.

An hour later, with take-out lunch from the breakfast restaurant in hand, we thought we'd have to use a shoehorn to squeeze the girls into a tiny corner of the truck. They weren't amused when I asked if I could take a picture of them.

We eventually found our way around the detours to the area in front the residence where parents had been asked to stop, drop and go (stop the truck, drop off all the student's stuff and leave to park the truck

ASAP to make room for the next packed vehicle). It was raining, which made the unloading a little trickier, especially with the few items that weren't packaged and protected from rain, such as the shaggy back rest and equally fuzzy mat for the floor next to her bed.

My husband and I unloaded the truck as our two daughters made their way to the second floor to drop the first few items off at Chloe's room. Fortunately, she wasn't on a higher floor, and we could walk up the stairs, because there was a long lineup for the elevator. They continued to carry boxes upstairs until we had unloaded everything and then my husband went off in search of the parking lot and each of us took turns guarding the goods, while the other two lugged stuff upstairs and made one trip up the elevator with a couple of heavier boxes and the mini fridge we had borrowed.

By the time dutiful dad returned, drenched from the pouring rain, we were already in the room, unpacking. Boxes were piled high and were even spilling over into the hallway. Strangers stopped at the door to shake their heads and smile in solidarity and others likely wondered how we were going to fit so much into her room.

Although my daughter had resisted taking the electric broom and mop, they actually came in very handy when cleaning the laminate floor (other rooms had vinyl floor or carpet, which I thought didn't look as nice). In addition, I had a bucket that I filled with warm water and anti-bacterial cleaner and set about wiping the shelves with wet rags, while the girls unpacked clothes and food items and placed perishables in the fridge.

When my husband and I left a couple of hours later to attend a parent information session (where we were able to scan a special code into our phones in order to sign up to receive the university's newsletter), the room was taking shape.

Our older daughter was helping her sister decorate the room and when we returned about an hour later, we were very impressed with the wall hangings and way in which the room looked extremely inviting. The floor-standing fan was whirring at full blast, since there was no air conditioning and what with the high humidity and fast paced movement while unpacking, things were heating up.

Another two hours (approximately four in total), the room was complete and my daughter agreed we could take photos of her on her bed. My husband had gone to get the truck in preparation for our departure. Once he returned, my daughters and I made our way downstairs.

We stood outside the residence and hugged goodbye. I shed a few tears and watched as Chloe walked towards the front door. As she disappeared from view, there was a horrible sinking feeling in my stomach.

As anticipated, it was difficult to get into the truck and drive away without her in it.

Turns out that staying another night in the hotel was a great idea. Not only did it give us a place to take a much-needed shower, but also an opportunity to relax and reflect, once again, on the day's events. Even though she had resisted us staying overnight initially, I actually think that there was some degree of comfort for our daughter, knowing that we were literally a few minutes away if absolutely needed.

That night in the hotel, as I lay in bed, about to turn off the light to go to sleep, I felt a wave of panic. Other than when my daughter had gone on a supervised trip to France in Grade 11, there hadn't been a day in her life until then that I hadn't known her exact whereabouts when I went to sleep.

I remembered her boyfriend telling us about an App that his parents used to 'track' his whereabouts. At first, I was a little ambivalent about this. I didn't want her to think that we were watching her every move. On the other hand, I knew that it would give me great peace of mind knowing where she was or that she was back at residence by the time I went to sleep.

I reminded myself (justified wanting it?) that by being able to see her location, I also wouldn't have to text a "where are you?" so often. Ultimately, I was glad she consented to me using this app and it certainly has been helpful. Although not every parent will feel the desire to check where their teens are most of the time, and some may have an easier time letting go, for me this was quite difficult. At first, I checked it almost obsessively, but as you will read, I became so much better at not doing so, as the year progressed.

THE MORNING AFTER...

We awoke around 9 a.m. The minute I opened my eyes, my first thought was "I survived the first night without knowing exactly where she was" (I didn't have the app installed at that time.) Then I checked my phone and saw that she had texted me at 1:40 a.m., almost eight hours earlier.

"It's so lonely here," she wrote, "it really makes me appreciate you guys. Thanks for everything and all your help." My heart felt like it was breaking.

A few minutes after waking, another text arrived.

"My fridge doesn't seem to be working. The dial inside was on '0'. I've turned the dial now, but I'm not sure how far to turn it."

I texted back that I was sorry to hear that she was lonely, but that it was normal for nights to be most difficult, especially at first. I then suggested she call me, which she did, and we discussed the dial in the fridge. I praised her for figuring out that the problem was with the dial, and asked how she had slept.

The bed, she said, was less comfortable than her own and the topper we had borrowed had made it a little softer, but not by much. Like a trooper, she said that she would likely just need to get used to it. She hadn't had much sleep, but had to wake by 6:30 a.m. for a 7:15 a.m. breakfast. Not wanting to eat so early, she settled for her usual peanut butter on toast before attending a morning lecture on consent.

She shared that she and a couple of girls from her floor had gone down-town the night before and that they had been stopped by campus police asking one of her new friends to get rid of the beer bottle in her hand. Although she had been part of the throngs of party revellers crawling the streets, maniacally celebrating, as if birds released from their cages, my daughter didn't sound as if she had loved being part of the chaos.

She said that students lifted other students up in the air on mattresses as others spiralled into frenzied states of drinking and partying all night.

Apparently, this is not unlike most first Frosh nights at any university.

I was glad to hear that she was not impressed by all of this. In fact, she was only too happy to escape the craziness after only an hour of being in the midst of it. I put that down to the fact that she had been experiencing increasing amounts of independence beginning in Grade 11 and then more so in Grade 12.

We were aware that she engaged in drinking and occasional pot smoking and although we didn't condone it, we did not condemn it, either. Our philosophy was and is to keep informed about what she is interested in exploring and then to try to make sure that she manages herself and her actions responsibly. Hearing her talk with such disenchantment about the party revellers made me feel that excessive partying was not something she had to get out of her system.

At a restaurant for breakfast the same day, even though the remaining three of us have eaten many meals without my younger daughter before, that morning felt different. We knew that this was going to be our new normal for a while. It felt like our four-legged, stable table had lost a leg and that our family was feeling a little unstable and wobbly.

After breakfast, we checked out of the hotel and then headed home. Leaving the city in which my daughter was living without us renewed the lump in my throat and created a feeling I had never felt before.

I tried not to think about leaving her behind and to adjust my thinking and attitude towards one of gratitude that we could afford to send her to university, that she had the motivation and ability to attend a post-secondary place of learning, and that she had the determination to pursue her dreams.

But still, at the same time, I allowed myself to feel the sadness that comes with getting used to not having someone who has lived with you for her entire life—that's 6,570 days if you choose to do the calculations. I also comforted myself with the knowledge that she would only be gone for approximately 190 out of 365 days a year and in total, only about 760 days over four years.

I know that I'm not alone in counting days, but more typically the days that are counted are those in the week leading up to a visit home for the weekend or slightly longer. For the purpose of helping parents who are feeling a greater sense of loss, perhaps these calculations will be of comfort, too.

SECTION THREE

FINDING YOUR WAY–
SOCIALLY, EMOTIONALLY,
ACADEMICALLY AND MORE

CHAPTER EIGHT

SETTLING IN
YOUR FIRST WEEK APART

Arriving home was a little strange. Again, even though we had walked through the front door many times without her, this time felt different. Walking into her room caused the sinking-stomach feeling again, so I closed her door and went to mine to unpack.

I remembered a conversation I'd recently had with my friend, Gary, whose child had moved into residence, five hours drive away, the week prior. He talked about the deafening silence in the house, especially now that his son was not around to play the piano. He said that "it's as if the soul of the house has gone".

A couple of days after Christine and her family had driven their son an hour's drive away to residence, she and I went for a walk. When she arrived at my house, we hugged for a while, as we both stood at the doorway, with tears running down our cheeks.

"I've never felt this way before," she cried. "I'm so excited for him because he's so happy to be in residence (she had spoken to him that morning as he woke to the sound of clanging pots and pans alerting students that breakfast was about to be served), and I know that this is the way that things are supposed to be, but I miss him so much already." I tried reassuring her, and myself, that every day would get a little easier.

As we set off for our walk, we bumped into my neighbour. We stopped to talk for a few minutes and somehow, perhaps as an outgrowth of her telling us about raising three now adult children, Christine shared her feelings about Ryan being away. As she spoke, she began to cry. "I can't believe this," she said to the neighbour, "I don't even know you and I'm crying like a baby."

My neighbour put her hand on Christine's arm and said "that's OK, I understand how you feel," and I guess she really did, because she, too, at this point was wiping away tears. So, there we stood, three mothers lamenting the absence of our children, united by understanding the courage that it takes for a parent to let go and to trust in their child and the universe that everything will be OK outside the nest.

Further into our walk, another good friend of Christine's, seeing us walking, pulled her car to the curb. She rolled down her window to ask us how we were doing and that's all it took for Christine to begin crying again. Her friend got out of the car to give her a hug and then, having seen two of her three children off to university and eventually back home again, tried to engage Christine in a philosophical discussion about how this is the natural evolution of things, that it was meant to be this way, that it was all good and that Christine should consider allowing her son to launch as a gift.

Of course, Christine and I already knew all of this. But this wasn't an intellectual response to a life-changing event. This was all heart. All emotion.

As we continued our walk (acknowledging that walking in one's neighbourhood isn't always the best way to get proper exercise), we comforted one another by remembering that this wasn't about moving out, per se—isn't moving out when you are financially able to pay your own way?—but about a temporary move not too far away and that we would still see our children with some regularity and over the summer months, for a longer period of time.

We paused for a few minutes in the playground area behind the school where our children had met years ago to reminisce about how quickly the years had passed and how many great memories had been created in that space in our neighbourhood.

That afternoon, Christine texted me from a decadent dessert place downtown. She had ventured there with her husband and 15-year-old daughter (who had begged her brother "please don't leave me alone with them!") to indulge in a specialty ice cream cone made from a sweet dough and filled with peanut brittle, peanut butter and pretzels, beneath soft-serve vanilla ice cream. "Emotional eating, lol" was all she wrote. I understood fully.

LATER THAT NIGHT...

I was up late catching up on some work, when I received a text at 1:09 a.m.

It read: "Help. I got a stain on my duvet cover."

The good thing about a white duvet cover is that you can bleach it clean. The bad thing is that it shows every mark.

"What made the stain?" I asked.

"I don't know. Maybe a drink. How do I get it out?"

At 18, how much does a teen really know about spot removal?

Not so simple, I thought.

She told me that it was the size of a quarter and that she didn't know what the red mark was comprised of other than "a drink".

"I just noticed it. People were in my room."

I went on to explain how to try to remove it with a Tide to Go stick and suggested that she buy a small container of bleach if that didn't work. I sent instructions about how to remove it carefully with the tip of a Q-Tip and how not to let the bleach touch anything with colour. Oh, the things they don't know they need to know until they really need to!

All of these instructions. Am I crazy? I wondered. Why am I indulging in this at such an ungodly hour, but again, the thought of my daughter being away from home and asking her mom (me) for help, made me jump to attention.

1:39 a.m. and another text: "my fan is making weird noises".

After we established that it wasn't a good idea to leave the fan running for 24 hours continuously, I suggested that she give it a break, and open a window. She replied, "But I'm gonna be so hot". I said that I was sorry, but I was going to bed and goodnight.

Unfortunately, after that I couldn't get to sleep. Last I checked my phone it was 3:45 a.m. and I was worrying about how I was going to get through a full day with client sessions beginning at 10 a.m.

Fortunately, when my alarm went off at 8 a.m., I wasn't feeling too tired.

I sent a text to my daughter to ask her how she had made out with the stain and she replied that it was almost gone. Good for her.

At 9:30 a.m., she wrote to say that she had been to the gym (another good for her), but that she was feeling sad because her nose stud had fallen out and she hadn't been able to find it.

"I feel very sad that lots of things are breaking and not working," she wrote.

I was tempted to say welcome to the real world, sweet pea, but I didn't. Instead, I acknowledged how hard it must be for her to be responsible for so many things, but that she was working out the kinks. I reminded her of the successes so far—getting her fridge to work and the stain out of her duvet, to name just two.

She texted again at 5:28 p.m. while out shopping for groceries with her boyfriend, after buying a new nose stud.

"Should I get a whole pack of lemons? They only sell packs," she wrote.

Fortunately, I was in a client session when the text arrived, so I couldn't rush to her aid. By the time I had finished and asked what she decided to do about the lemons, she said she had decided against buying so many. A conversation ensued about how to know when something is no longer edible and how long fruit lasts when refrigerated.

I am sometimes conflicted about how many answers I should give her and how much she should learn from trial and error. I remind myself that it's OK to guide and teach her along the way.

I feel nostalgic when I drive past my daughter's high school and see students walking around its vicinity. I remember her, too, walking across the road to the strip mall at lunch time or down the street towards our house. It is hard to believe that this phase of our lives is over.

Over the following few days, I spoke to some friends who were feeling very similar emotions to me, some with children who had also just been dropped off at university and another with a child in her first day of high school. We commiserated and cried together.

And my daughter did her fair share of crying, too. Nights continued to be the most difficult. During the day she was participating in the planned events, but at night, when the ghosts and goblins come out to play and make merry, she appeared to doubt herself and to question why she was not interested in squeezing her way into a crowded party house and drinking herself into a frenzy, as many of the students seemed to want to do.

One evening, her boyfriend was going to such a party and she was second guessing whether she should, too. She considered attending a quieter event, but then re-considered when she thought about going to her room at 11 p.m. and experiencing loneliness and solitude again.

Through our text messages, I encouraged her to try to be true to herself and told her that I didn't want to make the decision for her.

She had decided to step out of her comfort zone and take the plunge by going to the party after all.

However, just before leaving, she called to say how anxious she was feeling. I tried to help her manage her emotions, but she said that she was feeling utterly and hopelessly alone.

This was absolutely not what I had anticipated from my self-confident, socially comfortable, fun-loving teenager. In such a short time she seemed to have become a fragile, vulnerable person and I worried that she was bowing under the stress. I recommended that she speak to a counsellor at Student Wellness Services, which is open year round.

Along with this vulnerability, my fears were being realized in regards to her burning the candle at both ends. I was cautiously optimistic that she would flop into bed, exhausted from the day's events (and there are many) by midnight—OK, 1 a.m. But no such luck. I think the average time by which she was going to bed was more like 2:30 or 3 a.m. When you're required to wake up early for breakfast or activities, she was likely getting about three hours of sleep a night. Of course, sleep deprivation doesn't help when dealing with living the life of an adult overnight, along with poor nutrition or little food in her body.

The following evening, after a call from her at 11:30 p.m., I spent the following hour trying to convince her that of the thousands of new students, I was pretty sure that at least a quarter, or more, of them were crying in their rooms to their moms on the phone, too. I also wanted her to know that just because she didn't want to party all night and maybe throw up all over the sidewalk, did not mean that anything was wrong with her.

I finally convinced her to take a shower and get ready for bed (she complained she feels grungy all the time as the showers don't always produce hot or a steady stream of water). I was hoping that a good night's sleep would help her feel better, but my dreams were short lived and shattered by the sound of my cell phone ringing. I looked at it for the time—1:28 a.m. I answered knowing that it must be her. This was beginning to be a pattern. "Mom," she said, her voice quivering, "I don't think I can take this anymore. I want to come home. I'm not having fun. I feel like I'm just doing what I have to do, but I'm not enjoying it. Everyone else looks like they've adjusted."

I sat up, my head reeling from being woken and my brain put to work the second it became somewhat alert.

I wanted to get in the car at that moment and rescue her. I wanted to hug her and never let her go.

Instead I said, "sweetie, I'd like nothing more than to bring you home right now, but I think that would be unwise. This is the hardest week you will ever have to live through at university" (hopefully, I thought). "And I think you will be disappointed and regret it if you come home so soon." She was silent.

"You're right," she said.

The next morning, her nerves were frayed and she said that she was having a difficult time getting out of bed. I asked if she wanted me to come to her. No, was her reply. I asked if she wanted to come home for the weekend. No.

Despite being in such a fragile emotional state, she had the insight to realize that seeing me or coming home at this point in time would make it very difficult for her to return to school. She recognized that the following week would likely be better. Students would hopefully have gotten some of their wild partying needs out of their systems and things would settle down to a more reasonable level of activity.

We discussed how long Frosh Week feels and how it might be better if it was only three or four days long. By the time we hung up, I had convinced her to eat a little breakfast and to check out some more activities.

She called back around 11 a.m. She told me that she had plans to see her boyfriend later in the day, but until then, was at odds with how to fill her time. Although there were activities planned, she wasn't really feeling the energy or desire to be a part of them. I suggested that she take an Uber into town to get someone at a piercing shop to replace her nose stud, since she hadn't had any luck re inserting it. She said she was back in bed, but would try.

I was very proud of her when, an hour later, she called to say that she was on her way back from the piercing shop and mission had been accomplished. I commended her for doing this—for getting out of bed and for pushing herself to be outside and doing something productive. She was sounding a little bit better and I began to breathe a little better, too.

Amazing how, I thought, that even when our babies reach the age of 18 and feel that they can conquer the world on their own, what a humbling experience it must be to learn that complete independence may not be all that it's cracked up to be. Yes, learning how to rely on oneself is important, but counting on friends and family for support is not only important, but vital—at least until they feel more grounded.

WHAT A DIFFERENCE A WEEK MAKES...

It's hard to believe that it was only a week ago today that we said goodbye to our daughter.

It's been a tumultuous week for her and for the people who love her most at home, but especially me. I hadn't anticipated playing psychologist 24/7 and especially not in the wee hours of the morning, when she appeared on the verge of wanting to pack up and come back home.

But now, it appeared that she was settling down. A sore throat was the worst of what she was dealing with at that moment, so that's actually good news, because at least she can medicate a sore throat. A sore heart is so much harder to deal with.

She seemed to have had a great day yesterday. She even said that she was "good" when asked, which was wonderful to hear. After a full-out induction ceremony, complete with band and town crier, she and her fellow Froshers were formally welcomed into the university. Then she participated in a charity car wash and got ready for the semi-formal marking the end of Frosh Week—good riddance!

I spoke to her after she returned from an apparently not very well organized semi-formal. One of the problems was that there was nowhere to sit (standing and dancing room only) and so standing in heels all night was no fun. With feet already sore and blistering from slightly too big new high-heeled shoes, she and some new friends walked about 20 minutes away to the home of one of the Frosh leaders. Unfortunately, the leader had forgotten her key and so they had to walk another half hour to get to another Frosh leader's home. On the way, crippled by the pain from the blisters, Chloe took off her shoes and walked barefoot the rest of the way.

"You walked barefoot!" I exclaimed. Good thing I didn't know about it at the time. "Don't you know what you could have stood on? Glass, metal, anything!"

"It was the better of two evils, mom," she said. "I couldn't stand it one more second."

She took an Uber home—with her shoes on, thank goodness.

The idea of Frosh Week is exciting and scary for most students. Some get totally intoxicated as their self-proclaimed rite of passage, while others (the minority) observe or are more cautious.

What I came to know by the end of our first week apart:

- To expect the unexpected. I thought that my friendly, out-going, independent daughter was going to love being away from home and that we wouldn't hear from her very much. In fact, just the opposite happened.

- To be on call 24/7. For the first week at least. You likely wouldn't be able to keep your crisis line operational for too long, but be prepared to be on high alert at the beginning.

- To be patient and level headed—for obvious reasons.

- To remain positive and encouraging. Even though your teen might feel like he's the only one crying on the phone to you or that his world is falling apart, keep reminding him of his successes. Remember that with each hardship, he will be growing and learning and experiencing life like never before.

- To remember that with your teen away, there will be less laundry, fewer shoes to clutter up the front hallway and more leftovers in the fridge to choose from.

- To realize that there may be less conflict around the house (our girls are actually enjoying a better relationship living apart than together).

- To remember that despite what I have been challenged by this week, I feel less stressed and less like I'm walking on eggshells as a result of not having a teenager at home. I'm freer to be me!

- To recognize that I'm enjoying not being interrupted at 3:30 p.m. anymore. For so many years, unless I was away at the office seeing clients, I felt guilty when I wasn't giving the kids my full attention, once they were home from school. So, I always felt that my time was between 9 a.m. and 3:30 p.m.—school hours, in other words.

- That journalling is immensely helpful. I find solace in being able to record what's going on and I've encouraged my daughter to keep a journal of her first year, too.

CHAPTER NINE

NAVIGATING CAMPUS
THE FIRST MONTH

Sometimes I feel like I'm a GPS (Good Parent for a Student).

"Mom, I need your help," she said.

"I figure I should do some laundry tonight, but I don't know how to use the machine in residence. And also, can I put my towel and black leggings in with the underwear?"

I suggested she go to the laundry room and send me a photo of the front panel of the washing machine, so that I could help her decipher the options.

She sent the photo and I suggested choosing 'colours' out of 'options', which included 'whites' and 'permanent press'.

"What would I use permanent press for?" she asked.

Damned if I knew and neither did any of the friends I was out for dinner with.

"Don't worry about permanent press," I assured her. "I've not chosen that option in 30 years of using a washing machine, so I doubt you will either."

But you learn from experience and from asking questions, I reassured her.

My friends and I discussed how managing laundry is typically one of the most challenging aspects of living alone for the first time.

By the time that she had taken her clean clothes up to her room and was collapsing her laundry basket, she had called us on FaceTime to keep her company as she folded her laundry.

"Oh my god," she exclaimed, holding up her black leggings.

"Look what's happened to my leggings!"

The black leggings were coated with bits of white from her towel. The towel was being washed for the first time, so I'm assuming it was especially shedding its outer layer.

I suggested that she use her lint roller to get the pieces of lint off her leggings. She said she would the next time she wore them and folded them neatly to put in her drawer.

A friend whose son had attended the same university a few years previously, suggested that she put her dirty laundry in a bag with wheels and take it a laundromat close by (as her son had). There, they would wash and fold her laundry for only $5. While I filed the information away in my mind for future reference, if needed, I am wary of taking the gift of learning to do laundry away from her so soon.

The first Monday of her first week of class she had a one-hour lecture at 8:30 a.m. She arrived at 8:15 a.m. to find the hall almost completely full (not surprising for the first class of first year) and she had a hard time finding a single seat.

There was a technical glitch with the professor's computer, which delayed his introductory presentation by half an hour. He then offered the curriculum outline very dryly, showed a video and dismissed the class 10 minutes early. Not a very inspiring beginning!

Her next class was scheduled to begin at 2:30 p.m. Although it's not ideal to have big pockets of time between classes, I guess it's better than what she originally arranged for her timetable, which left no time between some of her classes. With classes requiring a 10-minute walk, or further away from the last, this would have meant arriving late for certain classes, which would not have made a great impression or helped her ease into things. So, she's left with this.

At least she has the weekend to recuperate before waking up at 7:30 a.m. on Monday morning in order to eat a quick breakfast in her room (if she does) and get to class in time (which may prove to be difficult because despite a week of orientation and frequently visiting her boyfriend on campus the previous year, she says she has no idea where any of her classes are and is relying on Google Maps to get her there). I wonder if not knowing where things are has anything to do with deciding not to attend the campus tour activity?

At 2:40 p.m. she called me. I was surprised, because class was supposed to have started 10 minutes previously.

"You won't believe this," she said. "I went all the way to class" (took her about 15 minutes to get there) "to find a note on the door saying that class had been cancelled and would resume same time, same place next week. What a waste of time! Why couldn't they have sent an email?"

And then, "What am I going to do for the next two hours?" she asked. "I'm bored."

I've noticed that it has becoming increasingly difficult for this generation of teens to tolerate boredom. Their brains are like snow globes, it seems, with thousands of specks of information to process all the time. With their constant overuse of cell phones, computer screens and video games, their brains are used to being in constant motion and the desire for more novel information is immediate. When the specks settle, they feel the need to shake things up a little so that they go back to their 'normal'.

I assured her that by the end of the week she would likely have lots to keep her busy. It was a beautiful day weather wise, so I suggested that she walk some more (she wasn't thrilled with that idea) or text a friend or two to see what they were up to.

At 3:30 p.m., she called again to see what I was up to.

She was quite obviously still bored, because she told me that she had just vacuumed her floor and was looking for the micro-fibre cloth to stick to the bottom of the long-handled mop so that she could wet sweep the floor.

"There are no cloths," I told her. "Just the one I bought the day before you moved in." The one I used to clean her floor, rinsed out and placed back on the mop.

"Oh no," she said, "I threw that out the first night."

"Why?" I asked.

"Because it was dirty."

I agreed that it wasn't as clean as when I took it out of its packaging, but that it was meant to be rinsed and used and rinsed again and then washed in the machine and used at least a dozen more times before throwing it out. At about $12 apiece, it certainly wasn't the same as daily contact lenses that get disposed of at the end of the day.

"So, what should I do?" she asked.

I suggested that she purchase another one the next time she went to the grocery store and in the meantime, use the handle to move a dampened piece of paper towel across the floor. This wasn't apparently very successful, so she opted to wipe the floor with paper towel in her hand. She was surprised to see how dirty the paper towel was afterwards.

I'm thinking that she may grow her appreciation for the work that is required to keep a home looking as it does when she walks through the door. She is already realizing that clean clothes don't just magically appear folded and without lint all over them and that floors don't stay clean forever—not even for a week—without putting some work into them being that way.

After wiping her floor, she went through her mini fridge and asked how she could tell if the cucumbers, for example, were still edible. I mentioned that they should appear firm, not squishy or slimy. Reassured that they were still good to go, she sliced a few pieces before filling her reusable water bottle and placing the cucumber slices inside it.

"I don't like this having to be responsible for myself all the time, mom."

I laughed, thinking that after we were off the phone, I was going to take a nap.

"You're going to be just fine," I said.

On the second day of class, and knowing that my daughter didn't have class until 10:30 that morning, I had planned on not calling to see if she was awake in time. But by 9:30 a.m., I called anyway and resigned myself to taking a couple of weeks to weaning both her and myself off my morning calls.

We spoke again around midday. She was in the cafeteria with an old friend from a youth group she had been part of all through high school.

Her first class of the day had been philosophy—a subject she had never taken before, but was quite interested in knowing more about.

She mentioned that it appeared that most of the other 200 kids in the class (the ones who spoke out loud anyway), had attended philosophy class before or were that way inclined because "they spoke so knowledgeably and it made me feel stupid. One person said something like: 'So if there is no universal moral truth, isn't everything a lie?' I can tell this course is going to be a real challenge," she said. "Not sure it's really for me."

About an hour later, she called again.

The problem of the day centred around note taking. And here I am again amazed and excited that she is actually asking for my advice, for my input and she's actually seeming to think that my ideas are pretty good. Yay for me.

"I realize that I don't really know how to take notes. I'm trying to copy the notes from the PowerPoint at the same time as listening to the professor, but I can't keep up. Do you have any tips?"

"Well," I said, "I just happen to be an expert at listening and taking notes. It's what I do with my clients at every session. I need to keep notes in their file, but I also need to listen carefully enough so that I understand their concerns and can follow up with relevant questions."

"So, give me some tips, then," she urged.

It took some thinking to break down the sequence of how I listen and take notes, but eventually I suggested to:

1. Take a picture of the PowerPoint image with your phone so that you don't have to waste time writing it down yourself.

2. Listen intently to the professor and then when he or she says something that sounds particularly important or relevant, write it down in point form. Another reason for the attentive listening is so that you can expand on your points later on.

3. In between classes or that evening (don't wait until the next day or you won't remember the details as well), type up class notes on your computer. You may choose to write out each point from the PowerPoint image, for example, and then expand on your own bullet point notes related to the PowerPoint points.

4. Print the page if you'd like, so you can file it away in a binder.

5. Practice makes perfect. Listening and recording relevant information at the same time is a skill that gets better over time.

"Any other problems we need to come up with solutions for?" I enquired. "Well, there is one," she said. "I signed up for the cheerleading squad, but I didn't know that there were going to be auditions to get in. They're tonight from 8:30 to 11:30 p.m. I'm not sure I feel up to it or if I want to compete."

I was of two minds. On one hand I wanted to encourage her to get involved, to meet more people and to expand her horizons. On the other, the phrases 'slow and steady wins the race' and 'don't take on more than you can chew', sprung into my mind.

Ultimately, I suggested that because this year—and especially right now—is a time of getting to know the campus, herself and is an intense period of adjustment to living alone and going to university, that she might want to defer something that likely requires a high level of commitment, to next year when she is better adjusted.

Again, she agreed.

One of the more difficult aspects of having your child live away from home is when he or she is not feeling well. It's normal to want to feel his forehead for a fever, or check out an unusual hive on her arm. So, when I received a text saying that my daughter's sore throat had gotten worse, I was concerned.

"I think I'm gonna go to the walk-in, but I'm scared because I don't want to get a swab," she wrote.

I called and reminded her of all the challenges she had overcome this past week and how I was sure she could conquer this, too. And I told myself that this was one more step towards learning to take care of herself.

My daughter found a walk-in clinic fairly close by. There were about five people ahead of her when she arrived shortly before 7 p.m. and she was told to take a seat.

She texted while waiting to tell me that she couldn't help but overhear patients announce to the receptionist the reason for wanting to see the doctor. "It seems that everyone in this waiting room suspects that they either have a throat or urinary tract infection," she wrote.

"Too much partying? Sharing of saliva and other bodily fluids?" I replied.

"Yep, exactly," she responded.

At the same time, another patient in the waiting room was apparently engaged in conversation with someone about how to break it to a guy that she had a sexually transmitted infection.

When my daughter finally met with the doctor, she asked if he was "bored" listening to the same complaints all evening. Not bored, he said, just wondering what was in the air, but thinking that it had something to do with too much partying and not enough rest.

Doctor's orders were to rest and drink lots of fluids and to come back for a mononucleosis test in a couple of days if she was no better. Although I wasn't happy to hear this, I figured that he was just being cautious. I'd known other people who had mono and wasn't convinced that her symptoms were extreme enough to be ultra-concerned.

Ultimately, her sore throat got better without any further medical intervention.

While walking back to residence, she picked up a sandwich for dinner. Not from the cafeteria, though, because it closes at 8 p.m.

My daughter shared that she liked her psychology class best so far, partly because her professor is so animated. She's trying to get used to sitting in a lecture hall as opposed to a classroom and said that waiting in line for the auditorium door to open felt like standing in a lineup for a concert venue with 500 other fans.

When seated, she took note of the incessant clickety clack of 1,000 hands typing on keyboards—taking notes—maybe! She said it sounded like the drone of insects in a hive and was distracting, but I'm sure it's a sound she will get used to and be able to block out over time (hopefully!). So far, she has not taken her computer to class as most other students have, but prefers to make hand-written notes.

After a couple of weeks into the first semester of first year, with most students already buckling down to review their notes, do their homework and with partying somewhat out of their systems (for now), my daughter no longer feels as compelled to leave her room every waking moment in case she misses out on something (FOMO or fear of missing out).

One night, as we were chatting, there was a knock on her door. Her new BFF had come to say goodnight.

"That's so nice," I said.

"It is," she responded. "It's something that we do. Say goodnight to one another."

I could tell that in time, she and her floormates were going to feel like family towards one another.

And having that sense of belonging is so important for all human beings.

I didn't call my daughter this morning as we agreed, but she called me.

"I felt weird again when I woke up this morning," she said.

"Weird? What do you mean by weird?" I asked.

"Well, my heart was racing and my stomach was sore," she replied.

It sounded like anxiety to me, but I didn't want to automatically assume that before asking some questions. We established that her room wasn't as hot as it had been.

She said that she felt better when she left her room, but worse when alone in it.

This sounded like anxiety to me, even though she's convinced that she's the only person feeling this way. I figure that she's feeling ungrounded, that the silence of being alone in her room when she first wakes is deafening. That she is quickly reminded of her aloneness and the intensity of having to do things all on her own is likely overwhelming.

I tried to normalize her feelings, but it didn't help that much.

"I don't know what I'm doing here," she said, "I just want to come home."

"To do what?" I asked.

"I don't know. I just don't want to be here right now."

I reminded her that this was not an option and that it was too soon to throw in the towel.

"When then?" she asked.

"When do you think?" I asked back.

"I don't want to set a deadline, because I will just be waiting for that time."

"Well, then, how would you feel if I said that you should ride out the year?" I asked.

"It makes me feel sad," she responded.

I acknowledged her feelings and tried to help from a distance. I knew that I could easily be sucked into her emotional vortex.

It appeared that her anxiety about staying in residence was about as strong as her fears about not returning to university after a visit home.

I think that part of her apprehension about not returning to university is because she's already seen some of her peers do just that. Not many, but a few. Ultimately, you've got to know your own teen and just how desperately depressed or anxious he or she is, but as a rule, if you can encourage your child to find the right resources at university (even if it means a short trip there yourself to provide moral support and guidance), if you can give her arm's length support to get through the first semester, at least, then things will likely improve as time goes on.

Katie Hurley, a Licensed Clinical Social Worker in the USA, and author of several books including *The Happy Kid Handbook*, says that while doing research for her teen depression journal – *The Depression Workbook for Teens*, available on Amazon as of October, 2019, she read that 31% of teens feel overwhelmed by stress; 30% of teens feel sad or depressed because of stress; and 36% of teens feel fatigued because of stress (American Psychological Association Stress in America survey, 2014). Hurley believes that "teen stress rivals adult stress" and implores parents to "check on your teens. They need you".

I told Chloe that I would indeed help by making sure that staying at home was not an option. I think she wanted to know that I was going to stand firm on this, because if I started to waiver, she would feel even less stable.

I then tried to distract her by talking about her upcoming plans. She had arranged to meet her new BFF for lunch and her old friend from elementary school days, for dinner.

I tried to assure her that what she was feeling was normal. I again suggested that she visit the counselling centre after lunch. I was thinking that if a university counsellor assures her that this is normal and that he or she has seen hundreds of other students ride out this storm, that she might believe it.

She said she would.

We talked about her coming home for a weekend visit in about 10 days. Again, she voiced her worry about coming home and then not wanting to return. I'm of two minds. On one hand, she has a point, but on the other, perhaps she just needs to come home for a bit as a reminder that we are not so far away.

It was 4:14 p.m. and I received a text (how did students and their parents manage to stay in touch before technological devices?!): "thought my class started at 4:30 but it started at 4. Oy!"

"Oy is right."

Less than 10 minutes later: "I don't have a good feeling about this."
"Why?" I enquired.

"The teacher is so boring and the material too."

I had tried to warn her that history might not be her bag, but she wanted to select it anyway.

"Well, I'm just gonna have to deal with it."

One part of me wanted to support this decision, concerned that she may be premature in deciding how bad it was going to be. Another part of me worried that the longer she remained in it, the more material she would be missing in another course, that she may want to switch into.

"Maybe this will be a challenge," she continued.

"A challenge? A challenge to stay awake?"

"Yes," she responded.

I suggested that if she was going to challenge herself to stay in the course, that she should challenge herself to listen even more intently, because if she continued to text me, she certainly couldn't do that.

I urged her to speak to an academic advisor about what to do and she said she would.

During our next conversation, she was excited to tell me about an amazing book that was bundled with her sociology textbook.

She sent me a picture of a page from *Kickstarting Your Academic Career*, Ostergard and Fisher, with the heading '*why am I here: from high school to college or university*'.

I could tell from the text I read why she had connected with it so well. It likely validated all that she was feeling by describing how overwhelming and daunting students find this big transition. I think it also consolidated everything I had been telling her over the past couple of weeks.

Even though she had not spoken to an academic advisor about her concerns and options (apparently upper year students had convinced her that it would be a waste of time), she had decided not to continue with the history course. She had replaced it, in semester one, with a course much more to her liking related to brain development.

Unfortunately, she wasn't able to find a course to fill the hole in second semester, though, and this was causing her a great deal of angst. Ultimately, she found a course that she could take online.

Switching into the other courses, I heard, was a fairly simple process that required some online navigation.

After an hour of back and forth discussion (and more shuffling of courses in the hopes of being able to finish classes earlier on a Friday or have no classes on that day at all—with no luck), we said goodnight.

Come Saturday night and she was feeling panicky and very lost again. I've come to understand that weekends on campus are also very challenging—especially when you're in first year. This is why many students, especially those who are living an hour or less away from home, return more often, even every weekend. This is not advised. The consequences are the same as for the high school student who comes home alone during lunch recess every day—if students don't connect with their peers during lunch, after class or on weekends in residence, there's less opportunity to connect with others and the less involved they are, the more on the outside they feel.

So, that evening was spent coaching her through feelings of anxiety and aloneness again and it occurred to me that not only was she coping with making new friends, but also with the loss of her old childhood friends who were scattered around the world.

Her latest worry was about finding housemates for second year when she will no longer live in residence.

There are so many pressures from all directions.

She mentioned the idea of perhaps attending a different university for second year that wasn't as notorious for so much partying. I reminded her that although the thought of going to another university where the vibe may be different seemed appealing, that there might be other difficulties to cope with, such as integrating into a second year of students who have already created cliques and made living off residence arrangements. That it may, in fact, be like going from the frying pan into the fire, so to speak, and that once she had seen her first year through, she would be much better able to cope (even enjoy!) her remaining years at university.

After that, she appeared to settle down again. Spending so much time contemplating another big move isn't good for one's soul, to say nothing about the amount of room it occupies in the brain of a student already trying to accommodate everything else on her plate.

What I came to know by the end of our second week apart:

- To continue to remain positive and patient.
- To pull back after the first few days and to not call in the mornings before class to make sure she was up.
- To encourage her to continue to be courageous and to face unpleasant experiences such as a throat swab on her own.
- To remind her that we are not very far away.
- To remember that I should continue to enjoy longer days and to focus on my own personal interests.
- That as much as I enjoy speaking to my daughter regularly, I ultimately want her to feel settled in enough so that I hear from her less.

Regardless of whether your teen is living away or commuting to their campus, many find it challenging when transitioning to a larger academic environment.

Being in a tutorial classroom with 25 students, as opposed to massive lecture halls with 500 people is more to my daughter's liking and most likely more to every first-year student's liking, because it's what they're used to in high school.

One of Chloe's fellow students actually approached her to introduce herself. That was a first, and I could tell that my daughter was thrilled about someone actually taking the initiative to meet her.

"See," I told her. "Only a couple weeks into classes and you're already making new friends."

Encourage, encourage, encourage has become my mantra. Finding opportunities to prop her up, to remind her of her successes and letting her know that I believe in her ability to confront and overcome challenges are so vital towards her being more settled.

When I arrived at my office one morning, I walked into a colleague's office to see a new sign hanging on his wall. It read: 'DIFFICULT ROADS OFTEN LEAD TO BEAUTIFUL DESTINATIONS'. In light of what I am helping my daughter deal with, this resonated with me. She is indeed on a difficult road, but I do believe that working through it with a little help from the people around her (including me) and even beginning a course of anti-anxiety medication to take the edge off her intensely anxious emotions, will help.

In the meantime, I sent her a card in the mail today. I think it's kind of nice to receive a card the old-fashioned way, through 'snail mail'. I'm hoping that all of these small gestures will go a long way to keeping her on track. When I went into the store to find a card, I wasn't sure what I was looking for. Get well seemed somewhat appropriate, but not quite, especially since the majority of cards in that section of the shelves were meant for those who were physically ill or in hospital. I finally found one in a tiny group of support cards in the Get Well section which said exactly what I wanted to say. On the front was a brightly coloured bird in an equally colourful tree.

The caption on the top read: "Never forget (not even for a second) you are amazing". Inside it read: "You have incredible strength, talent and optimism". And then further down "that's why I never doubt (not even for one second) that you can do absolutely anything".

I needn't have added anything more in my handwriting, since the card had already so eloquently expressed my sentiments, but I wrote a few lines about our belief that she would be able to persist though this period of adjustment and ultimately feel proud of herself for persevering.

Every day I am reminded that she is not alone in her struggle. One of my clients whose son also moved into a residence even further from home this year, shared with his mother that he had not met "his people". I was included in an email to several of my colleagues, mentioning the need for a counsellor in a specific university town for an 18-year-old male struggling with transitional issues (I didn't have to think hard to understand what these were about) and I heard about yet another recently university-bound student who was packing it in and returning home.

On a bad day, when my daughter was on the down side of the roller coaster (and I was feeling all that she was feeling, too) I sometimes wondered whether encouraging her to stay despite what she was enduring, was worth it. And yet, her words "please don't let me stay home" ring in my ears. When I hear her sounding positive and comfortable and too busy to speak to me when I call, I let my breath out and go about my day feeling that everything will work out well in the end.

Almost a month after her leaving, and in preparation for my daughter's first visit back home for the weekend, I washed her duvet cover, vacuumed her carpet and even painted over the areas of her wall where the paint had chipped off.

I also bought her a scratchable bingo card (she loves bingo) and a few goodies to munch on at home or to take back with her.

That night was strange not to have her with us as we observed a religious holiday. It would be the first without her since she was born over 18 years ago and firsts are always the most difficult to deal with.

She was feeling it too when she texted: "I'm really sad that I'm not at home ☹".

But she was home soon enough.

Getting ready for bed after her first day back, she commented on how good the water tasted (maybe it doesn't taste the same coming through much older pipes than ours?) and how grateful she was for two-ply toilet paper and for a towel to wipe her hands on (apparently there is nothing in the communal bathroom—not even paper towel—to wipe her wet hands on). She enjoyed taking a shower in a stall where she didn't have to worry about wearing shoes to protect her feet from picking up fungus, and eating "real" food (she devoured her steak). She enjoyed lying in bed with her cats at her side. And I believe she even enjoyed connecting with us.

I'm sure that the thrill of what she once took for granted will be short lived, but for the moment it was good to see the heightened level of appreciation for what she has at home.

It reminded me of part of the sermon the rabbi had given in synagogue a few days previously.

He spoke of a man who had travelled to a bridge in Vienna after having a dream of treasure there. Once there, he hung out by the bridge, waiting for a time where he could be least conspicuous looking for it. A police officer stopped to ask what he was doing and he told him the truth. The police officer made a comment about him taking his dream too literally and shared a dream that he, too, had once had about treasure under the cellar floor of a home he described in detail. He had done nothing about going in search of it, though. The man, recognizing that cellar floor and home as his, decided instead to return home in search of the treasure the police officer had dreamed about.

Of course, the treasure was there and the man realized that in order to find the treasure that was his the whole time, he had to leave home to learn about it.

What I came to know by the end of our third week apart:

- That three weeks is a long time apart, especially when you've never had to go through that before.
- To continue to applaud her for being more engaged in class and after. She is going to the gym with her friend more often and tried the dance class, too.
- That writing continues to prop me up and helps get feelings out.
- It's wonderful that family and friends continue to support me and it's good knowing that my daughter is growing her own support system away from home.
- To remind myself that she has worked hard to get where she is and to continue to stand firm in my conviction that it's too soon to abandon her journey, despite sometimes having to deal with sad and anxious feelings.

Now, 24-hours into her visit back home and it feels like she never left. At times I wish that she would never leave again and other times I'm pleased that she's not staying too long. Even though it is great seeing her in her own bed in the morning and seeing her face every day, I haven't missed being asked to leave her room the second I walk in, haven't missed her telling me what clothes I shouldn't be seen wearing out in public or seeing her clothes on the floor (I'm definitely holdng my tongue since she's only here for the weekend).

When we're not living under the same roof, I find that we have better phone and text conversations, but that changes pretty quickly when she returns and we all fall back into familiar patterns of behaviour.

While home, she reunited with many of her old friends, some of whom were in for the weekend for religious observances and others, hearing that their friends were home, made the decision to join them. They hung out together two of the three nights she was in, and shared stories with one another. It appears that at least half (likely more) of her old group of friends are struggling with the same concerns as her—especially in regards to making new friends and adjusting to their new living arrangements. Most were not having as good a time away from their families and parental nagging as they had thought. The grass is not greener on the other side after all. I think it was reassuring to know that what she is going through (even after everything I've said already) is similar or the same as most of her peer group. It helped her feel less alone.

Before she left, I found her flipping through a book I had left on the coffee table. *The Feeling Good Handbook: The Groundbreaking Program with Powerful New Techniques and Step-by-Step Exercises to Overcome Depression, Conquer Anxiety, and Enjoy Greater Intimacy* is one I often recommend to clients. David D. Burns, the book's author, is well known for his work in helping people develop strategies to change their mood by changing their thoughts and behaviour.

I asked if she would like to borrow it so that she could read it at university. At first, she seemed reluctant to take on another reading assignment, but I was able to help her realize the benefit of doing so. I suggested that she read a chapter each night before going to bed and complete the worksheets in the book. I was so glad to see that she had packed the book in her suitcase.

When it came time to leave, I could tell that she was feeling somewhat apprehensive and anxious, but the parting wasn't as traumatic as I think she imagined it might be.

It's as though she was climbing a ladder and just when she got to a higher step and was out of breath, she rested (came home). By doing so, she was able to take time to sleep (in an air-conditioned room and more comfortable bed), have others prepare real food and nurture her, and this gave her the energy to keep going with renewed motivation and determination. Who would have thought? And we were worried about her not wanting to return.

When she arrived back on campus, she texted to let me know that she had vacuumed and cleaned her floor along with other surfaces and was on her way towards washing her sheets.

I was very happy to hear about this (especially since she had left her bed at home unmade, her nightgown on the floor and the laundry basket on top of her unmade bed). I did remember, however, on the first night she was home, her mention that she was upset that she hadn't made her bed before leaving university…that she would have preferred to be welcomed by a neatly made bed.

So, it made sense to me that she wanted to put her nest in order upon her return. Still, I asked about her motivation for digging right in, and she said that she wanted to create an orderly environment in which to do work. I saw this as progress and another sign that coming home may have been just the right thing for her after all.

Since returning to residence and taking pride by cleaning and organizing her space, she seems more settled in, more comfortable with spending time alone than before.

Last night she went running with a new friend. She's never gone running, but said she really enjoyed it.

I was also thrilled to hear that she was applying to work as a volunteer at a distress line at university, because as I well know, often when you help others, you help yourself.

She also scheduled and attended an appointment at the writing centre where someone (who told her she switched her major four times) helped her properly format the first writing assignment she'd just completed.

She attended a special dinner for her residence (each residence has one during the year apparently) where she ate "real" food and got to know people she hadn't yet met, even though she's been living in the residence for over a month. This helped to remind her that she's not done meeting new people and making new friends—not by a long shot.

She's signing up to take part in different psychology research projects by upper year students so that she can earn extra grades in psychology herself, and in general, is getting more involved on campus.

The word anxiety has barely come up in conversation over the last few days and it appears that for the most part, she is enjoying being in residence a lot more than before she came home for the weekend.

My daughter reported that there was a break in the heat and it was wonderful to feel a cool breeze while walking outside. It was apparently still quite hot in the old building she calls home, but I suspect that she will sleep better tonight.

And I am sleeping better knowing that she is doing better overall.

She is continuing to develop a network of people to whom she can go for support and with questions. Maybe not to ask if she can still eat bread that is stale dated, or what to do with a stain on her duvet cover, but since these practical kinks are being ironed out, she can settle into the real reasons she is there—to learn, but also to grow emotionally.

It makes me happy when she talks about plans for next year—a couple of weeks ago she didn't even think she was staying for the remainder of this year.

I tell her how proud I am of her (and how proud she should feel, too) for all the support systems she has put into place for herself and we discuss the benefit of creating a community of caring.

What I came to know by the end of our fourth week apart:
- That I have come a long way in this long-distance parenting arena.
- Even though I want to know where she is throughout the day, I resist the urge to check the "tracker" app.
- That the more my daughter shows comfort and ease living away in residence, the more I relax and get comfortable with her living away from home.

- That her continued openness about her daily activities is as a result of how we are responding to what she shares with us. I am being very careful to pull back and to allow her to experience the consequences of her behaviour that I'm not happy about (missing class and staying up too late, for example). Instead of reprimanding or lecturing, I am acknowledging her feelings. In fact, I am working a lot less hard by only advising when I am asked and the rest of the time just validating what she is sharing.

- More and more (even as a result of talking to friends and clients in the same boat as me), I have come to realize that this generation of university and college bound students, so used to getting information instantly at their fingertips, think that if they haven't made friends and settled in by the end of the first week or two, that they are losers and outcasts. I am continuing to assure my daughter that patience is a virtue and that she is only about three percent into her four years and still has 97 percent's worth of time to meet people and to adapt to her environment.

CHAPTER TEN

CHALLENGES AND CHANGES UNTIL CHRISTMAS BREAK

I was curious about how my relationships with the mothers of my daughter's friends might change, not having car pool, homework assignments, homeroom teachers and our kids crazy-making behaviour to discuss. Turns out, the friendships have remained pretty solid with most, and we don't just talk about our kids anymore (although they do still feature heavily in our conversations).

Over lunch, Daphne, one of the friends I met through my daughter, and I, calculated the number of days—26—since the girls had moved into residence and reflected on how much had happened and changed over such a short space of time. On one hand it feels like they left yesterday and on the other, that they have been gone forever.

Regardless, we concluded that things were moving in a positive direction, that we expected some zig zagging along the way, but that we were sure that the girls would continue to thrive and grow.

Another friend and I exchanged thoughts on the pros and cons of students living alone in residence rather than sharing a room. Her daughter had requested a room in residence with a good friend from high school and it had been approved. At first it appeared like the best decision. However, now that a month had passed, she regretted not requesting a private room. She was feeling constricted by being in the same space all the time. She wanted more breathing room and longed for her roommate to go home on occasional weekends, which she rarely did. By contrast, I shared that my daughter sometimes felt lonely on her own.

In the end, we concluded that while it was very personal as to whether a private versus shared arrangement was best suited for the individual student, that living alone may have more pros than sharing—for our girls, anyway.

Her daughter, I found out, despite very much enjoying the business program in which she was enrolled, was actually considering switching to a university closer to home for second year.

Turns out that they are on the same roller coaster ride as we are, and so are the many families I've spoken to and heard about over the past couple of months. And just when we think that the highs and lows are over and the ride has ended, we're back on and encountering different highs and lows all over again.

My daughter was anxious about meeting the counsellor at university. She was worried about what to say. I suggested that she share her anxieties with him and I am hoping that he will not only normalize her experience, but will also offer her some coping strategies.

The session apparently went well. The counsellor referred her to a program that combines personal training with anxiety management. Sounds like a winning combination—especially since she's long wanted a personal trainer and because working out will help reduce her anxiety and increase her feeling of wellbeing (working out releases feel-good chemicals called endorphins).

As hoped, he also offered her some strategies for feeling better when she first wakes in the morning and validated her experiences until now as being "normal". She plans on seeing him again and I'm glad for this.

After a great evening with her boyfriend, some delicious food and a good night's sleep, my daughter appeared to be in a positive mood.

At 3:35 p.m. she said she was just chilling.

At 7:43 p.m. she sent a text saying: "Not sure what to do tonight. Everyone drinks and stuff and I'm just not in the mood".

I acknowledged her desire to fit in and reminded her not to give in to peer pressure (I know she knows this, but sometimes, as parents, we say what we need to say in order to feel that we are doing our jobs right).

My husband and I went out for dinner and when we got home at 10:30 p.m., I wrote to ask if she was OK. Her text back took me by surprise.

"DRUNK" was all she wrote.

"Seriously?" I texted back.

I wasn't sure whether to believe her or not, especially after her text a few hours earlier.

"Yes," she responded.

I took some degree of comfort in the knowledge that she had shared her condition with me and that she at least wasn't drunk enough not to be able to text. However, "DRUNK" sounded ominous. Why not "drunk"? That would have been bad enough.

So, I did what any 'good' parent would do.

I asked questions to make sure that she was as safe as she could be under the circumstances.

"Are you in res?" I asked, hoping she was close to 'home', and "who are you with?" hoping she would provide me with some of the names of people I'd already heard about.

And then: "thought you didn't want to?"

Her response was half reassuring: "people on my floor". OK. So at least she was steps away from her room. I didn't have to envision her staggering from another residence to her own. I didn't have to worry about her falling down drunk on the ground with no coat on or being alone while vomiting into a garbage can or on the ground.

In response to my "thought you didn't want to"…she texted, "I did".

OK, then. Not sure what changed her mind between 7:43 and 10:30 p.m., but something did.

"Still drinking?" I asked, with the words 'alcohol poisoning' piercing through my brain like a neon sign.

The neon sign dimmed slightly when she answered.

"No."

Perhaps they'd run out of alcohol.

"Well, can you FaceTime me at midnight?" I asked, hoping I could see her to assess the damage. As far as I knew, this was her first time getting DRUNK away from home, so I wanted to make sure that she was somewhat more sober by then.

Her honest response: "Maybe".

OK, maybe not, I thought was more likely.

It's 12:28 a.m. I'm still awake and no further communication from her. I sent her another text "u OK?"

A minute later: "Yes. Just drunk ☺ ".

Ok. Just "drunk", not DRUNK, was an improvement. But what was up with the smiley face emoticon? I figured that meant that she was happy about her predicament. Oh no.

"I'm with people. Talk tomorrow and don't worry, I'm not drinking anymore." "Ok g'night," I wrote, resigned to the fact that I wasn't going to be seeing or speaking to her any time before going to bed and realizing that I may have pushed things a little too far.

I came to realize that my daughter (still a few months underage at the time) sometimes drank alcohol so that she could feel more relaxed in an environment that makes her uncomfortable. It's not the alcohol she enjoys so much, but the ability to feel more relaxed in a somewhat inebriated state, and especially if others are, too. As a parent I struggle with this.

As a psychologist, having spoken to many teens over the past decades, I understand the need and desire to fit in and the lengths that teens will go to in order to make sure that they do.

We didn't turn off our light until around 1 a.m., so we were still asleep this morning at 7:11 a.m. when my husband's cell phone on his bedside table rang.

I heard him say "what's the matter?"

I knew that at a call from our daughter at 7 a.m. on a Sunday morning wasn't a good sign.

He spoke to her for a couple of minutes before handing his phone to me.

She told me how badly her head hurt.

I wanted to say: "serves you right. I hope you've learned your lesson," but I knew better than to say that.

I knew that the consequences of the hangover would hopefully be lesson enough and I didn't have to say anything.

I established that she had drunk mostly vodka and that she had already taken Advil, but had hoped it would have taken effect since 20 minutes had passed.

I suggested that she wait a little longer and to call us back if there was no difference within the hour. I also suggested that she drink a lot of water that day so that she could rehydrate.

It's 12:23 p.m. and my daughter texted to say that she was awake and her headache had gone.

Her peers had apparently woken before her and the halls were pretty deserted with fellow students either at breakfast or outdoors enjoying the beautiful crisp fall day.

She was on her way to pick up lunch.

Depending on the home in which you were raised, and the rules or opinions that you heard (from the parents you maybe swore you'd never be like), along with your personal beliefs about alcohol and drug use, your teen's behaviour may be different to your friend or neighbour's teen, when it comes to being honest with you. For example, if your teen knows that although you don't condone underage drinking, but that you understand peer pressure and are open to talking about responsible drinking, then he or she is more likely to talk to you about what is happening at parties and less likely to lie or drink behind your back.

The same is true when it comes to recreational drug use. Experimentation does not mean that your teen is a 'bad' kid or that he or she will become a drug addict. I know that many parents fear this and I understand your concern, but my belief is that it's far better for your teen to see you as being approachable and open, rather than believing that they need to keep a tight lid on what they're doing when you're not around.

The upside of my daughter's boyfriend being one year ahead of her was that she was somewhat more familiar with the layout of the campus than other new students, when she moved into residence. She was excited at the prospect of having someone she could count on living so close to her. However, they both came to realize that having a boy or girlfriend attend the same university is not always ideal.

As her first year unfolded, they found it challenging to juggle their activities on campus and with their friends, along with their academics, while still making time for their relationship.

And while they navigated this, others around them were finding their way with different partners—some more discriminatingly than others. Universities do their best to promote safe sex and to offer resources and paraphernalia (such as condoms, but also lubricant, dildos and butt plugs, for example), but whether a student chooses to practise safe sex is, of course, up to them.

Living in residence (or away for the first time at 18) may be a ripe situation for sexual promiscuity. As my daughter says, "you have your own room, full privacy" and even for those who are sharing a room, there is an unwritten rule that when you want to have someone over, your roommate makes him or herself scarce—one becomes "sexiled," in other words.

If teens are raised in homes where sexuality is talked about openly and respectfully and if parents understand normal and healthy sexual development, there may be less risk of teenagers rushing into sexual exploration and experimentation the minute they are out of their parent's sight.

So, now is not the time to be bashful about having honest conversations about safe sex, because insisting on abstinence or turning a blind eye is not very helpful.

My daughter had been informed that there would be a fire alarm drill sometime this week between the hours of 5 and 7 a.m. She knew the consequences of not getting outside as soon as possible and had prepared clothes to throw on quickly.

The students in her residence had been given an unofficial heads up the night before that the alarm drill would happen the next morning and whoever leaked the information was correct. The alarm went off at 5:45 a.m. and they were fortunate that the weather conditions were tolerable during the 20 minutes that they waited outside while rooms were checked and officials gave the all clear that it was safe for them to go inside…and back to bed.

Later, I called and found her with her boyfriend in a very long lineup along with many other students, all of whom were eagerly (and patiently) waiting to reach the front of the line at a beaver tail food truck. For those of you who aren't familiar with the edible Beaver Tail, it's a flat piece of dough, shaped like a beaver's tail, then deep fried and sprinkled with lots of sugar—just the sight of which typically raises my blood sugar levels.

No wonder my daughter ran (as in exercise run) to her friend's residence that night where they worked out some more and then had dinner together in what she described as a much nicer, more intimate cafeteria and a nice change from the long lineups she typically endures at the cafeteria in her residence. We spoke upon her return. She had apparently taken the bus back "home".

She assured me that doing so is perfectly safe and that she doesn't need to Uber from one residence to another. I'm actually getting to feel better about this and continue to encourage myself to envision a safe, busy, well-lit environment in which she is living and walking alone at times, rather than allowing my mind to wander to dark places.

My daughter sat with us in the living room upon her return home just before Thanksgiving weekend. I offered to slice some strawberries for her and put them in yoghurt. She was excited. "I can't remember the last time I even saw a strawberry," she said.

Later, after she had settled in—aka dumping her bags in a heap on the floor of her "nice clean room" (her words)—and was preparing for bed, she seemed upset. I asked what she was thinking about. She told me that she was having the same "weird" feelings that she had when she first arrived in residence. But even weirder for her was that she was experiencing them in our home.

We talked about the 24-hour changing direction adjustment period, as I like to call it. It's the same experience that children and parents in divorced situations typically find themselves when the children go from one home to the other.

At home, in spite of looking forward to the quiet and calm of not being surrounded by residence floormates 24/7, the quietness was too loud. She said that she was used to being busy all the time in residence, used to hanging out with her peers and going from room to room in the evenings. Here she was sitting in the burbs feeling like a bump on a log.

By the following morning, she was feeling much better. She and my husband were bopping around the city and enjoying a meal at a new restaurant he had scouted out for them. By the evening her weird feelings were gone and she was off to a bingo hall with her sister and some friends.

Yes, even she and her sister were on more civil terms, despite daughter number one's agitation at her sister for scooping the last bit of mint chocolate chip ice cream and not leaving enough tuna salad to put on her bagel.

One of the highlights of my daughter being home was partaking in the sharing of a 22-pound turkey at our friends Christine and Brent's house, as we reunited with other parents and teens from high school, for Thanksgiving.

Along with eating a delicious meal, we sat around enjoying having our kids with us. It was not only wonderful to see them all together again, but to catch up on news of their other friends—those who have spread in different directions and have reconvened this weekend—and the new ones they have made in residence.

Some of the stories made our hair stand up on end and while we were grateful to hear all the details, we listened with a kind of morbid curiosity to tales of sexual promiscuity, use of illicit drugs and partying escapades.

Other topics were more benign, such as the difference between a food-court eating area that one of the teens has at his university versus the cafeteria type at my daughter's university, or how eccentric some professors are (one apparently climbs on the desk and sits cross legged as he responds to students' questions with "that's a great question. Anyone else want to comment on that?") and how impossible it is to keep up with the 50-plus pages of reading per class each day (most students apparently don't even try).

After the adults were stuffed and falling asleep, not from the company, but from the high dose of tryptophan thanks to the turkey, we bid each other adieu to make space for our teens and their friends, more of whom had arrived. Since they were honest enough to admit that they were going to be drinking, we agreed to pick my daughter up by 1:30 a.m.—according to her, a much earlier time than she would end her partying on campus.

As I lay in bed, at least glad to know where my daughter was and who she was with, I reflected on how things change when she's in town. For one thing, life is much busier, because although she's only one of four of us, she's the one who wants to be on the move the most. So, the days are longer and the night activities more frequent. In addition, we turn off our lights a lot later and fret more about when she's going out and coming back home, what she's doing and with whom.

Most parents, us included, say that for some reason, we worry more about what time our teens will be home and where they're going, when they're back home under our roof. Perhaps because when they're away, we are not waiting up or sleeping with an ear open for when they come through the door.

It's challenging, I find, when she comes home, to find the right balance between continuing to parent and guide, while not rocking the boat for fear of not making the most of our short time together.

In counselling sessions, I hear from parents about how much their spousal relationship changes when kids, no matter their age, are around. When the kids are at overnight camp or away at university or when couples are away on holiday without the kids, they don't find themselves embroiled in the same confrontations surrounding the kids. There's no need to protect one's child from his or her other parent's harsh words, no need to jump to the defense of a spouse when one's child is being belligerent or disrespectful. No disagreements about which behaviours are acceptable or not and about how to discipline. And so, things are naturally calmer. Understanding that this is normal, anticipating these changes, and then figuring out how to adjust accordingly, is extremely important.

While driving my daughter to the train station when it was time to return to residence, I noticed that she was particularly quiet.

I touched her hand and asked what was troubling her. Close to tears, she shared how anxious she was about returning back to residence. How she still wasn't convinced that she was right for university and how worried she was about her mid-term exams for which she said she didn't know how to study.

We talked about making use of the school's resources as she has done at other times and I suggested that we chat again when she was back in residence to come up with strategies for studying.

"Try to keep your eye on the prize," I suggested.

"What prize?" she asked.

"The prize of leading a fulfilling life, doing what you want to do after you've finished your schooling," I said.

I know that it's so hard to project into the future. It's like suggesting to a student in Grade 9 that they choose a university to attend in four years time. In addition, when taking an undeclared bachelor's program (as many students do) with courses quite similar to what they took in high school, it's hard to really project oneself into a career of choice. If your teen has chosen an entry-level program, as my older daughter did when she chose graphic design, then there's not as much thinking that needs to go on in first year in regards to the major or program the student wants to focus on in second year and beyond.

By the time the train was half way back to university, she texted that she was feeling much better.

The following day appeared to be brighter. After the long weekend, her Tuesday timetable was less busy than her Monday would have been, and she spent the majority of her day connecting with other resources, such as the personal trainer that she'd been matched with as part of a prescription exercise program to which her counsellor had referred her.

She was also advised of an interview this week for the distress line volunteer position to which she had applied and learned of a paid social media position for her residence about which she is quite interested.

She wrote to tell me that, sadly, someone had stolen the white board on which she and others wrote with an erasable marker, that was taped to the outside of her residence door.

I think she was not only disappointed that it was gone, but that someone on her floor (she presumes) would have taken it.

I wondered if it was a prank, but regardless, it wasn't a kind gesture, especially when you're trying to build a community of trust.

Some of her peers had not yet returned to university because they had been given a Reading Week following Canadian Thanksgiving weekend.

Even though the university that one of her friends attended, had previously not scheduled that week off in October, I wonder if the reason they'd given this now is not because the students need a week away from academics yet, but because many universities have by now, seen an increase in the number of distress and suicide calls.

An October, 2017 article in *The Globe and Mail* newspaper, entitled Peace of Mind: universities see spike in students seeking mental-health help, cited findings from the "National College Health Assessment survey, a 2016 North American survey, which included responses from about 44,000 students from 41 Canadian post-secondary institutions." It concluded that "A fifth of Canadian post-secondary students are depressed and anxious or battling other mental health issues, up about 3 to 4 per cent from 2013" and "Another troubling finding is the percentage of Canadian students who indicated seriously contemplating suicide – 13 per cent – which increased by about 3.5 per cent from 2013".

I'm thinking that it would be of benefit then, for students to get some TLC from their families, and for parents to keep a watchful eye at regular intervals throughout the year, and especially during their teen's initial adjustment period.

After his lengthier period at home, Ryan's mom and dad (our friends, Christine and Brent) and his sister, made the trek to return him to campus. When they arrived, they helped him pack up the summer clothes he would not be needing, so that he could make room for his winter gear. When it came time to say goodbye to the son they'd only said goodbye to less than two months earlier, Christine felt heart sore. She said that there was a camaraderie and "I know exactly how you feel" looks exchanged between the departing parents as they ascended the stairs of the residence, and moved towards the parking lots and their waiting cars.

Homecoming Weekend at the university looms ahead with a big question mark above it. My daughter is anticipating it with a combination of dread and excitement.

The morning after Homecoming was officially in full swing, she called at 8:30 a.m. to say that she was up and already feeling ill from consuming beer, along with pancakes at 7:30 a.m.

Nevertheless, she was on her way to her boyfriend's fraternity brothers' 'kegger' at which she swore she would not drink more, only watch others getting drunk and possibly making fools of themselves.

The partying was apparently nonstop, and even more frenetic and overwhelming than during Frosh Week. Signs such as 'you honk, we drink' hung out of windows of houses in the student 'ghetto' and alumni of all ages filled the streets, drinking and being rowdy.

Eventually, she found her way to her boyfriend's house for an afternoon nap before venturing out to another house party with him.

If the students measure the success of a Homecoming Weekend by the number of drunk-related police charges, then I'd say that it surpassed the tip of the measuring tool. According to a news feed I read the day after, there were 330 charges laid and 33 arrested. Apparently, 307 of the charges were for violations such as having open alcohol, underage drinking and public intoxication. These charges were almost double the 166 laid the previous year. So much for Frosh Week being the peak of partying. She hadn't experienced anything like this before. Apparently, it's common knowledge that students donate blood prior to drinking. This apparently leads to getting drunk more quickly, which translates to not having to spend as much money in order to do so. How creative of them! I guess it's a boost to the blood bank, but I worry about how much of this then gets transfused back into students who have gotten into enough trouble to require an infusion of fresh blood themselves.

The Dons (typically upper level students who are placed in a leadership and advisory role to students on their floor) in the residences are apparently on high alert during Homecoming Weekend. Having non-residence friends stay over is a no-no, even though I'm sure that there's a fair amount of sneaking in.

During Homecoming, 'bars' (or badges of honour) are awarded to students for participating in specific mischievous pre-determined behaviours (none of which are condoned by the university) such as gathering with friends and Grey Goose vodka, pouring 50 shots and finishing them before a movie ends (affectionately referred to as '50 shots of grey').

When my daughter and I spoke later on the phone, she was trying to find some refuge in the student centre, but even that usually tamer area, was crowded and noisy.

When I spoke to my daughter the following morning, she was eating breakfast in her room—rice cakes and peanut butter have become her staple—before leaving to begin training for the distress line.

I remembered that they were providing lunch for the trainees.

"I think I'll take a couple of snacks, too," she said.

Every time she shows signs of taking care of herself well, I feel more inclined to pull back a little, knowing that she is in good hands—her own.

Later, after training had ended, we spoke briefly in between my client sessions. She sounded as though she'd had an enjoyable day, but could not share details with me because everything is strictly confidential, as it should be.

We also talked about the mark she'd received on a sociology assignment and she said that her plan was to book an appointment with her TA (Teaching Assistant) to figure out where she had gone wrong and how she could get a better mark next time. Atta girl!

Despite a long day, she had dinner in the cafeteria with some of her floormates and later was on her way to a house party. I was glad to hear that she was spreading her wings and interacting socially with different people.

I know I'm not the only parent to impress upon their teen to call a taxi or Uber rather than walking a long distance late at night alone. One night, at dinner with our friends whose daughter is away at another university, we compared notes about identical conversations with our daughters, during which they told us that the reason that they didn't want to keep calling an Uber or taxi service was because they didn't want us spending money unnecessarily. Kind of them to be so considerate, but we parents told them the same thing—that you can't put a price on safety and that we'd much rather spend the money knowing that they were not in harm's way.

It's another fine line we walk as parents. Not wanting to have our children see the world as an unsafe place or letting our anxieties hold them back, but also figuring out how safe they really are when walking alone at night.

Areas around universities and colleges are typically set up for safety. Most have poles with blue lights and a button which can be pressed to call security. Most also have walk-home programs so that a student can call on a couple of other students to walk them to or from residence or to another location on campus. The problem is that most teens feel that they are invincible and that no harm will come their way. Or they may be embarrassed to call on such a program because they don't want to be seen as afraid or needy.

My older daughter and I decided to take a road trip in the fall to visit her sister for a girls' weekend. I packed an overnight bag for me and a small suitcase entirely comprised of items our university daughter had requested, including a container of freshly baked cookies (my husband's contribution to the weekend away).

I suggested bringing a boot tray on which to put her wet boots when the winter weather hits. She liked that idea. However, I challenge you to find one that is suitable for a small room in residence. Not sure why, but the smaller versions that were so available when I last bought a boot tray (many years ago), are no longer available. I scoured our neighborhood by going in and out of at least six stores—from the local dollar store to the intermediate and big box stores—in my search. An hour later, I purchased a typically sized one for our house, so that I could replace one of the smaller mats I had at home that I intended to give to her.

This, along with more toiletries, food items, duvet clips to keep her duvet from moving around inside her cover (which it does more than mine ever has), will be included in the baggage. Oh, and yes, her winter coat, which I asked her to take the last time she returned to university, but she didn't.

When we arrived, I began unpacking the small piece of luggage. First thing out was the container of cookies.

Before long, word spread and a group of my daughter's floormates were at her door, eager for something homemade.

Before attempting to attach the duvet clips to the inner part of the duvet cover to keep it in place, I suggested that my daughter wash her duvet cover (since it hadn't been washed since moving in and likely wouldn't be washed for a while longer, especially with the added hassle of duvet clips to take on and off). Despite not wanting to deal with the crazy congestion of the laundry room at prime time (Saturday afternoon), she agreed that it made sense and besides "my sheets smell kind of funky—like vegetables". We stripped the bed of sheets, pillow case and duvet cover and then, she and her sister made the long trek down three flights of stairs into the smelly, warm bowels of the building so that she could load them into a machine.

While they were gone, and at my daughter's request, I got to work vacuuming and mopping the floor, and wiping down the very dusty counters. Aside from the dust bunnies, which were more the size of fluffy clouds under her bed, and the over-filled garbage cans, the room was not too dirty or untidy.

I had worn the t-shirt Chloe bought me for my birthday which had the words 'University Mom' on it, so I lived up to my definition of mom by making sure that I helped her out while in town.

Then she and her sister relaxed on the bed, catching up on a Netflix show, while I continued to organize and discard items that did not seem to be serving a purpose (of course, I checked this out with her first).

Later, as we heard fire engines outside, she asked "hear that?" We certainly could.

"Someone just pulled the fire alarm in another residence. It happens every day. It's almost always a false alarm."

Later she read us a post on one of their university's Instagram pages. It was from another student living in residence in the building to which the fire truck was called. Apparently, in response to the fire evacuation, he literally had to drag himself out of his sick bed (he had mono), clinging onto the railing, trying to make sure that his legs didn't give out beneath him. His message was addressed to the fire alarm puller and implored him or her to consider how some people—either sick or disabled—had to deal with this event. He wanted the prankster to know that the prank wasn't funny.

Half way through the show the girls were watching together, there was a knock on her door.

A floormate asked: "Did you say that you have a mop? Can I borrow it?"

Apparently, my daughter is the go-to person for everything—large and small—a paper clip, safety pin, bandage, cookie tray and now, mop.

She says she likes being helpful, so it wasn't a surprise that she was quick to loan the mop to her new friend.

I reflected on how much better my daughter is faring living in residence than others who may be more territorial or don't like to share. This is not to say that people who don't like to share or work as a team won't adjust to living in residence, just that it may be more difficult.

When her floormate brought the mop back, the micro-fibre pad was absolutely filthy.

Apparently, she had loaned it to another couple of people before returning it and I don't believe the pad was washed out between uses or after.

I wanted to say something about it being nice for people to return items in the condition they were given them, but bit my tongue, not wanting my words to impact their relationship.

Her floormate at least acknowledged the state it was in and muttered something about washing it the next time she did her laundry, but I offered to just throw it out. She seemed relieved.

My daughter had set a reminder beep on her phone to let her know when the washing cycle was over and so when it was time, I offered to accompany her into the basement so that I could visualize the surroundings when she said she was in the laundry room.

Down the stairs we went on sticky floors, past crumpled cans, discarded banana peels and shards of toilet paper like streamers, strewn down the hallways. There was a stench of alcohol. I asked my daughter if the halls always looked this way and she said no, mostly on weekends when there's no one to clean up after the students in their common areas.

In the laundry room, complete with a clogged sink and only about four washers and dryers to service more than 300 students in my daughter's residence, a female student with tousled hair and wearing sweatpants and shirt, sat on a small sofa, looking downwards at her textbook, highlighter in hand. She didn't look up when we entered. I wondered if she was as diligent a student as she appeared, or if she was seemingly absorbed in her study material as a way of distracting herself from having to engage socially.

A couple of guys were chatting as they removed clothing from two washing machines. They were dressed casually in shorts and t-shirts, with long socks and sandals. My daughter waited patiently for them to clear the way so that she could have access to one of the two machines that were then seemingly available. A few minutes later she came over to tell me that she would have to come back "later" because they were still using both.

I struggle to understand why there is no system in place. Why aren't the students able to sign their names onto a waiting list of sorts whereby they are assigned a washer or dryer in the order they arrive? Presently, it seems that if you're not like a vulture hovering over a machine the second it becomes available (and even then, you may not be secured a machine without a fight), that you never know when you'll be able to wash or dry your clothing.

My daughter is skeptical that anyone would stick to a system, but I figure it's worth talking to her student representative about.

It took a couple more trips back downstairs before she was able to wash and dry her sheets and covers, so that we could put everything back together before leaving to go out for dinner in the steadily pouring rain.

Before leaving to go out, I went to the co-ed bathroom (this is not typical in all residences) down the hall. Large enough to park at least two cars in, I noticed that the shower that had been running since I first washed out a rag in the sink at least two hours previously, was still running. At first, I thought someone was showering, but my daughter says that it never shuts off.

In the sink were discarded Cheerios, since the students wash their plates and cutlery that they use in their rooms in the bathroom sink. The garbage cans were overflowing with stinky containers that the students obviously preferred not to leave sitting in their rooms, (one mom said that she was told by her son, in residence at another university, that the janitor had punished the students by not replenishing toilet paper after they filled the washroom garbage cans with garbage from their rooms). The toilet paper felt lesser than one ply (I guess a student could bring their own) and there was no paper towel on which to wipe my hands after washing them (I was warned about this by my daughter).

No wonder, I thought, that my daughter is so much more appreciative of our soft toilet paper, clean living environment and always accessible laundry facilities.

At least, I comfort myself with the reminder, living in residence teaches one about greater appreciation and about the ability to develop resilience, taking turns and living and working alongside many different people with varying personalities and habits.

As Chloe says: "university changes people".

That evening, after a delicious dinner with the girls at a restaurant downtown, we walked back to the hotel where we were staying. My daughter was torn between going to a raucous fraternity party that her boyfriend and his brothers were hosting, or chilling with us in what might be considered a relatively boring evening at the hotel. I suggested that she could do both, that she could even take her older sister to the party, but in the end, she decided to just hang with us.

I'm not kidding myself by believing that it was our great company that she was really after. I think she's still feeling confused about where she prefers to hang her social hat. She's also confused about the changes she's experiencing in herself. Again, I am reminded of the independence she experienced before leaving for university and how she may have less of a desire or need to spread her wings so wide.

With only a few hours left to spend together (my daughter had another distress line training day until 2 p.m.), we forfeited sleeping in so that we could join her for breakfast before she headed out. She appeared sullen, which I presumed was because she would have much preferred to have slept in on a rainy Sunday morning in a comfy hotel bed than go to a training course.

Then she said, "I can't believe it's going to be another three weeks before I see you again," and I realized that thinking ahead (consciously or subconsciously) to saying goodbye was likely contributing to her mood.

Then later, after checking out of the hotel, we met up with a landlord we had been put in touch with at a house that was going to come available in time for my daughter to begin second year.

Chloe was meeting us there.

We had known in advance that the house had seven bedrooms and that my daughter wasn't thrilled at the prospect of living with six others, but I wanted to meet the landlord and to see one of his properties.

He had alerted the students living there, in advance, and they may have tidied the common areas in preparation for our visit, because other than the mounds of shoes in the front entrance, it was in relatively decent condition. Some of the bedrooms were messier than others, but my daughter seemed more able than me to overlook the mess and seemed excited at the prospect of living in a homey environment in second year.

This wasn't the house that my daughter ended up living in, but it was helpful to see it as part of our research.

As of yet, she hasn't decided who she'd like to live with. She has several people in mind, but none who complete her vision of what living in a house with other students is about. She's apparently heard stories about the people you're living with becoming lifelong friends, of becoming godparents to each other's children, of being each other's confidantes. So, her expectations are pretty high.

Later on, as we were saying goodbye, I had the feeling that my daughter was experiencing one of those "don't leave, please go" moments. "Please don't leave me alone with people I barely know, in a building that smells like alcohol and decaying banana peels" but "please go so that I can get back to studying for my midterm and to doing what I want when I want."

Ten minutes later, we received a text from her. It read: "Miss you ☹".

It was sent six minutes after we'd left.

On October 30 and eight weeks since my daughter moved into residence, the university hosted a parent evening at a large theatre in Toronto.

We were amongst at least another 150 parents of first-year students from different faculties, including arts & science, and engineering.

They were generous enough to provide complimentary water, soft drinks, tea, coffee and snacks.

The dean of student affairs welcomed us and spent the following 20 minutes offering us tips about how to help our teens develop resiliency (especially when handling disappointment) and how to continue to make sure that our children—their students—were on the path towards success.

She stressed how big of an adjustment and transition going from high school to university is and how challenging it can be for students to find their way and to learn how to regulate themselves when they are mostly used to being regulated by others, mostly us.

Then, once in residence, she explained, they have to learn the fine art of time management and self-regulation over many facets of their lives, including when to go to sleep (apparently 65 percent of their students reported feeling sleepy during the day!), how to make sure that they are up on time for class, how to take care of themselves by monitoring how much they eat and exercise to stay physically and mentally healthy, how to take care of one another, how to balance academics with social activities and how to guard oneself against the social pressures imposed by seeing postings on social media that can leave one feeling as if he or she is the only one sitting alone in their room at night.

It's exhausting just listing all they have to take care of, I thought, let alone managing it themselves (no wonder, along with staying up later than ever before—much of the time as a result of being on technology or partying—they're sleepy during the day).

She spent quite a bit of her presentation on the social aspect of residence life and was quick to mention that although they don't want to stop students from partying, or even drinking, that learning to self-regulate around using alcohol or drugs is a vital part of being healthy and successful, too.

She made mention of binge drinking (drinking more than 4-5 drinks at one sitting)—almost half of all their students reported binge drinking at least once in the previous two weeks—and the impact on their community neighbours as a result of unruly behavior and on the emergency department at their local hospital during special events like Homecoming.

She said that their focus is to promote the responsible and safe use of alcohol.

The previously mentioned 2016 online survey (National College Health Assessment—NCHA) that my daughter's university, along with 40 other Canadian institutions participated in, provided "an up-to-date picture of student health and wellness" across Canada.

Not surprisingly, the survey found that within the previous 12 months, more than 20 percent of their students who participated, said that they had been treated by a professional for anxiety and 15 percent for depression. This is consistent with what I see in my practice in regards to the top two mental health concerns that individuals present to me and is in keeping with what my daughter has experienced herself.

Interestingly, more than 83 percent said that they would seek help from a mental health professional if they had a personal problem that was bothering them. This was very encouraging and indicative of how much less of a stigma seeking help for personal problems is, especially by this age group (50 percent of respondents were between age 18 and 20, with the median age being 20). I am concerned that there may not be enough counsellors to see them all regularly, and in a timely manner, too. I've heard that it often takes a month or more to see a counsellor and then students sometimes wait as long for a follow-up session. With this in mind, I encourage students, and perhaps parents, to speak up when or if they feel that the waiting times are too long or that they are not receiving consistent care.

The report also indicated that of the students who completed the survey from their university, 79 percent had used alcohol in the past 30 days, 20 percent had used marijuana and seven percent cigarettes. Furthermore, almost nine percent had taken a prescription drug not prescribed to them.

Only 16 percent of their university's first-year respondents indicated that they had never used alcohol.

This information confirmed what my daughter has been sharing with us about the tremendous peer pressure surrounding alcohol consumption and re-affirmed my commitment to promoting responsible alcohol and drug consumption both personally and professionally. Helping our teens learn how to stretch a bottle of beer over a longer period of time, effectively tracking the number of drinks they've consumed and learning how to decline a drink while still feeling a part of the party are difficult topics to tackle, but so important to be discussed without judgement or criticism.

Aside from their obvious concerns about self-regulation, the university presenter offered parents other tips related to academic success.

Although I have written previously about my decision to allow my daughter to self-regulate regarding attendance at class, the presenter was specific about parents encouraging their teens to "go to class" and to "stay on top of their reading and study habits". She also encouraged parents to reinforce their teens accessing support services at the wellness centre, as well as meeting with academic advisors and professors, during scheduled office hours, to get extra help or guidance.

Results of the NCHA survey indicated that of all the issues their university students found difficult to handle, academics topped the list (61 percent) with sleep difficulties coming in second at 36 percent.

The presenter noted that top of the emotional and social stressors at that time of the year was looking for houses in which to live and with whom and that this could cause a fair amount of "drama" as well as social pressure about finding the right group of people.

We were reminded that students only had days before being able to drop any of this term's classes without any penalty on their transcripts and that they had until next May to choose to specialize or major in (with a "majors" night being offered during the first week of March, manned by students in that particular major, so as to make their selection process easier).

After we were divided into sections based on the faculties that our teens are in, an associate dean offered more information specific to our daughter's faculty and we learned more about other options, such as taking part in a paid internship program for 12 to 16 months, typically co-ordinated between years three and four, so as to offer the student work experience, an opportunity to be exposed to a potential career choice, and potentially an added incentive for a future employer to hire him or her after graduation.

The presentation ended with the dean of student affairs supporting us with the knowledge that we will not be judged for calling in for clarification or guidance on the way that university systems work. However, that students are encouraged to try to work things out for themselves first and that we wouldn't be given information about them specifically, unless our teens had given them permission to do so.

Further support, we were reminded, could be found on the parent support page of the university's website, as well as through their monthly parent newsletter, which we signed up to receive on my daughter's move-in day.

Halloween was different this year without my daughter in town. Even not having her home to hand out candy (she hasn't been trick or treating for years) felt different. It was a fairly typical day at school, she said, aside from a few students who went to town with creative costumes.

When we spoke that evening, I could hear that the door to her room was open (I noticed that this is common on most residence floors when I visited), because there was a lot of chatter in the background.

I like that she keeps her door open some of the time when she is there. Staying behind a closed door promotes social isolation and may lead to a less fulfilling residential experience.

I even noticed that some students had placed their pillow where others had their feet, so that their heads were facing the door. I presume that's so they can easily see people as they walk by in the hallway, if they're sitting on their beds.

A couple of girls who my daughter had never met before, but who she believes are residing on the floor below her, came trick or treating in reverse. Instead of her doling out candy to them, they came with treats for her and all the other residents in their building. Another great way to meet people and make friends!

It's mid November now.

Getting a 75 percent on the midterm for a class at which she is more absent than present, has likely encouraged my daughter to keep sleeping in on Wednesday mornings past its 8:30 a.m. start time. I have mixed emotions about her doing fairly well despite her lack of attendance, but keep my thoughts to myself.

On the flip side, she appears to be working much harder on assignments, reading and other homework than I have seen in a while. After deciding that her dad is better at helping her critique assigned reading (she says I'm better at editing her written work!), she has allocated reading material to him over the past few days.

The most recent email to which more reading was attached read: "Hi again. I know this article is very long, so you're allowed to say no, but I'm having trouble putting what this article talks about into a concise number of words, and why it's relevant to the first article I showed you on the topic I selected. If you have any insight, that would be much appreciated. So, here is your poop time reading material and food for thought for the day ☺ Love Chloe".

My husband and I were on our phones in bed when the email came through at around 11 p.m. He laughed out loud and read it to me. Now, how could he say no to such a politely written request? The humour added was just a cherry on the top.

"I'll read it tomorrow," my husband responded, after validating her sharing that "this is hard work!"

"Yes, it is hard work," he agreed. "But who said anything about university being easy!"

As always, we are both conscious of not doing the homework for her, but certainly don't mind offering our support, insight and direction from a distance.

~

It's actually quite surprising that she's able to get much work done this past week while inhaling the stench in the hallways and washroom. As I've mentioned before, there are no janitorial services during the weekend and the students know this and put up with it. One week, however, when Monday came and went with still no garbage removal, and as the washrooms became filthier, some students began to enquire as to why. I was told by my daughter that the janitor was off that week and hence, no cleaning or garbage removal.

Although I believe that the students can clean up after themselves, what about the overflowing bins and which student is going to clean the toilets, especially if they're too gross to sit down on? And why weren't they at least advised that there would be an interruption in service? Why did there need to be an interruption at all? Yes, people go on vacation, but surely there are others who can fill in, especially when it comes to sanitation and health.

Reminder to self: call the university to find out why this happened. Especially when we're paying good money for our kids to live on campus!

And speaking of health, my daughter is aware of at least two other cases of mono on her floor this week. One student has apparently gone home, but the other is battling his way through it. Reminds me of day-care days when being exposed to others' germs and contagions was part of the package and to be expected. The only difference is that hopefully these bigger kids will have a little better immunity than back then—that is as long as they are getting enough sleep, eating well and taking their vitamins—as if!

And in the midst of hard work, she's becoming even more concerned about who she will live with next year. Her good friend, from elementary school, has signed a lease with three other girls in her residence and my daughter and her new BFF have mutually concluded that they may not be compatible as housemates. So, the hunt is back on.

She's approached a guy friend in another residence about rooming together, as well as a female student who is in one of her classes, and she even responded to an unknown student's Facebook post about looking for one or two other students to live with. As of now, it appears that everyone is wanting to keep their options open rather than committing to anyone, out of fear that something or someone better will come along. Added to the anxiety of not being able to find a suitable house (as close to campus as possible being a top priority), and of being left behind as leases are signed, the pressure continues to mount.

As a postscript to what I wrote earlier, I called the facilities department at the university about the lack of janitorial services and asked why there was none. They were surprised to hear my report and assured me that even though one of the janitors was indeed on holiday, that there were others on the team, and that they would send someone by the next morning to inspect (not sure why the Don on the floor didn't do this as easily). However, just two hours later, I received a text from my daughter: "U rock mom. The washrooms have been cleaned!" Super (helicopter?) mom to the rescue!

⁓

I can hardly believe that in just over two weeks, my daughter's first semester will be over and exams will begin. I've just posted a podcast on my website about how to study for tests and exams and I'm hoping that some students will take the time to listen, because I think they will get a lot of value from it. As of now, my daughter hasn't expressed any worry about exams coming up. Some kids will ruminate about them for weeks ahead, and others, like my daughter, will start preparing when they're at her doorstep. No right or wrong, I believe. As long as she continues to remain motivated and level headed when managing her studies, I'm comfortable with letting her take charge. I'm also maintaining realistic standards, realizing that most students will see a dip in their grades from Grade 12 to university. I work at helping my daughter remember that ultimately, even though a good overall grade average is important, especially if she's planning on applying to a post-graduate program, that the pressure to be perfect is certainly not worth becoming emotionally or physically ill.

Right now, she's more concerned about making sure that her assignments and written papers are up to par and more importantly, that she's made sure to have thought them through critically and that they make sense.

Last Thursday night, after a very disappointing steak dinner (apparently students were lined up for at least 10 minutes waiting outside the cafeteria for their single piece of barely edible meat), she joined us on the phone, and my husband and I helped her fine tune a paper she'd written. First, I helped her edit for grammar and sense. There was very little to do, although I did notice that some of her paragraphs were verbose. "What are you trying to say?" I asked. She laughed. "I'm saying that I'm trying to add sentences to make the assignment appear longer!" Then she and her dad debated some of the issues she had written about and with his help, she modified it.

My daughter has come back home for the weekend again. She provided us with her food order before returning. On top of her list was filet mignon wrapped in bacon. Her boyfriend, who is in town for the weekend, too, was eager to join us. We've even offered to take them to a movie after the homemade dinner, since I don't believe she's been to a movie theatre since leaving in September.

We picked a recently renovated theatre in which we were able to pre-reserve luxuriously padded fully reclining seats. It felt even better than watching TV in our living room. The movie, about a young child born with a disfigured face, centered mostly around his experience with Grade 5 peers at school, following being home schooled until then. Before his first day, his parents suggest some "rules" to follow. My daughter, lounging on the chair next to mine, leaned over to me and said "How come you didn't share the rules of university before I left so I'd know what to expect?"

"Because," I whispered back, "I didn't know them."

I've printed a copy of her bank account so that together, we can reconcile the transactions at some point while she is home. With the grants she has received, the payments she has made to the university independently and the books and other items she has paid for, I feel somewhat in the dark about what funds are still available for next semester, so I figure it's time to sit with her (not really looking forward to this!) to try to make sense of it all.

Even though we were getting along well, I'm aware of how we get along even better when we're living apart. After a disagreement, for example, we have time apart to simmer down. I don't have to deal with my frustration about her constant cell phone use or not being able to approach her unless the time is right.

Once home, she shared her concern about more and more of her peers signing leases for houses to rent as of next May (rent typically has to be paid throughout the summer to hold their spot, even if there's no one living there).

She was feeling relieved to have heard back from the person who had created a post on Facebook looking for additional housemates and will be meeting up with her and two other already selected students, when she returns to residence. She says she's not feeling ultra-confident, because she knows she is just one of many candidates and she's not sure if she will present herself as well as usual, since she feels pressure to impress them.

While at home, after my daughter and her friend had gone to a restaurant for breakfast, she and I headed out to buy her new winter boots, a few long-sleeved shirts (she swears she doesn't have "any") and some new socks—hers are threadbare, she says.

After visiting our neighbour and friend, we went home for her to pack her small suitcase (I have no idea how she fit everything in it), along with more goodies such as homemade cookies and a loaf of freshly baked banana bread with chocolate chips, which my husband had made for her to take back to share with her friends.

She was planning on having an early dinner, but we ran out of time because she literally had to catch a train, and so she grabbed a few snacks and we headed out of the house.

It didn't take quite as long as predicted to get to the train station, so we had a half hour to wait before the train arrived. The station was under construction and it was dimly lit and cold when we arrived. She said she was fine navigating her way to the track, but there was no way that I was going to let her traverse the desolate looking station alone.

While waiting, my daughter admitted to feeling sad again. She said she wasn't sure why, but that the feeling had just come over her and she didn't like it. We explored her sadness a little more and I was reminded, once again, how transitions are tough. She said she wasn't looking forward to going back to residence and that the month ahead seemed long. She wondered out loud if any of her floormates would even have noticed that she had been away.

We talked about how the first year of being at university or college is a lot like being in Grade 9 again, but even harder because unlike Grade 9, which is typically experienced alongside some familiar faces and friends of many years, the first year of university is not only in an unfamiliar setting with unfamiliar teachers and increased responsibility, but most significantly, does not come with the infrastructure of support from trusted friends.

Things always seem worse in the dark and since this was the first time that my daughter was travelling by train alone (there's usually a friend or her boyfriend heading in the same direction), it was perhaps magnified by some anxiety related to that, too.

When the train finally arrived, we took her to the car she was assigned to, gave her a big hug and waved goodbye.

Before she even had time to find her seat, it was whizzing past us.

I walked away with that sinking feeling in my stomach, and reminded myself of the 24-hour changing direction adjustment period.

Turns out that the light of the following day didn't lift her spirits completely.

She was again feeling a little "lost", alone and sad. This, despite reconnecting with her floormates over banana bread and homemade cookies. I assured her that she had overcome this feeling before and would overcome it again.

When we spoke that evening, she sounded much better. She had met with the three girls who were looking for two more housemates for a place very close to campus. Apparently, they met in the cafeteria for dinner and then, when ushered out as it was closing, my daughter invited them to come back to her residence.

She felt a great connection with all of her prospective housemates and so was feeling a lot more optimistic than before the meeting. The house they have in mind is being renovated and will be ready for July, which gives them a break on rent, since they wouldn't be paying as of May, as is typically expected. The rent was fairly reasonable too—$600 for each of them, plus utilities—and for her room maybe slightly less rent since they asked if she would be open to sleeping on the main floor in a slightly smaller room attached to the kitchen.

She was a little unsure about this at first, but ultimately concluded that there may be more good than bad about living on the main floor (easy to bring her furniture in and out, not having to lug laundry up and down more stairs from the basement laundry facility and close to the common areas).

Despite the strong rapport she felt, the girls didn't give her a clear yay or nay in regards to whether she would be chosen. Fingers crossed.

We talked briefly about her plans for the evening and about upcoming exams. She is looking forward to increased mandatory quiet time in residence. Apparently, around now is when the quiet time, which is typically from 11 p.m. to 7 a.m. on weeknights, gets vastly extended. This way, students are not distracted by sounds of partying in the hallways and other rooms. This will be the students' first experience with exam prep and exam writing at university, so it will be interesting to see how that unfolds.

LAST WEEK OF SEMESTER ONE

My daughter texted me today to ask if it was OK to sign up for a psychology cram course. Not knowing what that was, I asked about it, including why she was asking me for permission.

I should have known it was because there was a cost involved—$120 for a crash course that covered the entire semester's curriculum over 12 hours at a downtown hotel.

As she explained it, this crash course, offered only for particular subjects, allowed her 12 hours of focused attention and study. No, it wasn't just meant for students who didn't know the material, she said. It was really a review of everything by someone who knew the material inside out (apparently, he'd offered 57 such courses to hundreds of other psychology students before her).

Since she had apparently allocated 15 hours towards studying for this particular exam (I was impressed that she had created a timetable), this opportunity meant that her studying for it would likely be done by the end of the 12 hours (six hours on Friday evening and the remaining six the following day). I gave her my blessing.

Just in time, prior to the end of classes, and students becoming completely absorbed in studying and writing exams, four girls, one of whom she'd never met before, plus my daughter, met over dinner one night to formalize their living arrangements and to make sure that they all felt equally compatible and comfortable about being housemates for year two (and beyond, hopefully).

I was excited to hear how the meeting had gone, and so when she texted to say that she was back in her room, I called.

"So?" I asked.

"What?" she asked.

"Is it official? Do you have a place to live next year?"

"Yes," she said, very casually.

I believe I was more excited than her. Perhaps because as a parent I could finally rest assured that she no longer had to worry about whether or not she would be left out and whether or not she would find a place close to campus. She, on the other hand, was probably sick and tired of how long this had dragged on. It was likely anti-climactic, after being interviewed weeks before, waiting for their response, and then meeting another housemate. I got it.

As a result of the house apparently being in a state of disrepair, she decided just to look at the blueprints, but not see it in person. We, on the other hand, thought it unwise to move in completely sight unseen. I suggested that she, her dad and I have an opportunity to meet with the landlord to scope out the house and especially her room, before she signed the contract (what experience do most 18-year-olds have signing contracts?), especially since we are the ones paying the rent.

I suggested that she arrange this meeting on the day of her final exam, before we drove her back home for a two-week break over Christmas and New Years. I first communicated this request via text, but she did not respond. I gave her the benefit of the doubt, knowing that she was in the midst of writing final papers and preparing to study, and hoping that she would understand where we are coming from.

WHACK A MOLE

I wondered if part of the reason that she hadn't responded to my text is because our phone conversation last night didn't end off too well. After discussing the living arrangements, and that the house allowed for one parking spot on the driveway, she informed me that she wanted to take the car that she and her sister share to fill that spot next year.

It feels that no sooner have we whacked one mole on the head and have it out of sight (such as where she is going to live next year), so another mole pops up (taking a shared car to university next year). Sometimes, those moles are stubborn and keep popping up no matter how many times you whack them down.

She was surprised to read in the lease that if they were to have a pet in the house—cat, rabbit or even hamster, for example—that there would be an additional $40 charge for rent of said animal per month.

Since some of the housemates are apparently allergic to cats, which would have been my daughter's number one choice, she wondered if they would still have to pay for an axolotl, which they are now considering as their creature to care for. No, we didn't know what an axolotl was either. That is, until we googled it and learned that it is a Mexican walking fish or salamander-type creature. It actually made me feel kind of squeamish to look at, but is apparently, to them kind of cute.

CRAM BEFORE AN EXAM

Despite the Psych 100 TA recommending against cramming for an exam, and even though many of the people who had initially expressed interest in joining her for the 12-hour cram session (most backed out because they thought it was too expensive and I was glad that she expressed appreciation at being able to take part), my daughter attended the first of her cram session on Friday between 4 and 10 p.m.

By the time it was done for that day, she was, too. In hindsight, taking a cram course towards the end of a weekday and into the night is a difficult task.

I hoped that she would have gotten a fairly early bedtime and I think she had planned on this too, especially considering that the second part of this cram session was beginning the following morning, but that was unfortunately not happening. Despite the 22 out of 24 hours a day of mandatorily imposed quiet time leading to exam day, one of her floormates, in particular, had drunk a few too many and apparently was not into following rules. My daughter was not happy, to say the least, especially when she hadn't quietened down by 2:30 a.m. Chloe's alarm was set to wake her five and a half hours later.

Even though she could have reported this to her floor Don (wasn't he supposed to be monitoring this anyway?) in the hopes that he would get the situation under control, she chose not to. "I don't want to be that person," she told us. And I understand. As tempting as it might be to get someone else to get the job done, when you're going to be living with the same group of people all school year, you've got to develop a whole lot of resilience, patience, tolerance, compassion and ability to co-exist with others, some of whom you wouldn't choose as friends.

When we called at 8 a.m. on Saturday morning (just before her cram course), as per her request, she said that yes, she was indeed up, but barely. Nevertheless, she managed to make herself a quick breakfast and to be in a taxi by 8:40 a.m.

I wasn't surprised to hear that she was having a difficult time staying awake, and wanting to leave by lunch break. Even though she thought that the instructor was mostly very interesting and relatable, and that she likely had a head start on studying for her psych test, that this would not, as she once thought, replace the need for studying for it. What she liked was that the attendees had all been given a thick package of notes to review and study from. She also learned that had she responded to a request, when the psych course started, for someone to attend each and every class, to take good notes, and to submit them to the organizer of the event, that she would have made $50 and could have attended the event for free.

On the next day, being Sunday, she's hoping to sleep in a little and then buckle down to more studying, since exams begin in five days.

Apparently, it's recommended that students' study nine hours a day, from 9 a.m. to noon, 2 to 5 p.m. and 7 to 10 p.m. and then sleep. Begin again the following day…

Along with sleep, which is a rare commodity for most students, I've also recommended that my daughter make sure that she eats nutritious food and gets enough exercise (which she has become really diligent about). In fact, if she had it her way, she'd trade in her peanut butter for organic almond butter, but in the meantime, so long as she's mostly dependent on cafeteria food, she says that she, along with other students, are just eating to live.

The quality and choice of cafeteria food is apparently different depending on which university you are attending. Most students are part of a meal plan and at least don't have to worry about food preparation and where to go to eat it, taking some of the stress away during a year of adjustments.

At first, my daughter said that they mostly offered burgers, pasta, ham and pizza. Over the course of the year, she became more creative and aware of what else she could request. So, despite being aware that most first-year students gain at least 15 pounds during their first year (coined 'Freshman 15'), she actually lost weight. This was partially due to making healthy food choices, but also because she was doing more walking than ever before and was also going to the gym.

In the meantime, some of her peers have gone home, especially if their first exam is a week or more away. Since hers is less than a week away, she's concluded that she will get more work done if she stays on campus.

Besides, she was looking forward to taking part in the Secret Santa event on her floor the following evening. It seems that the spirit of Christmas is revving up. Christmas themes have sprung up around campus. So that she has an opportunity to share some of her own traditions with her friends, she's invited a few people to her room during the week so that they can light Hanukkah candles, spin dreidels and eat chocolate gelt.

SCRAMBLED EGGS AND SCRAMBLING FOR A SEAT

In their psychology class, while learning about memory, the students were given some tips about how to be successful at studying. One of these was to study especially during the hours that the test is going to be written. With this in mind, my daughter's plan was to be particularly diligent about studying between 9 a.m. and noon, the time during which she will be writing her first university exam in three days.

She woke this morning with vim and vigour (well, maybe not quite!) and made it to the cafeteria for scrambled eggs and other breakfast items.

This was quite a treat since it was the first time she'd eaten breakfast away from her room since the start of the school year. She was quite surprised at how delicious it was, so maybe this will be part of a new tradition or at least a reason to get out of bed a little earlier for the remainder of the year.

After breakfast, once most of the students had left to find a space in which to study (most don't study in their rooms, but seem to prefer to congregate together—perhaps for inspiration in the same way as one might go to a gym to work out rather than to the treadmill in one's basement), my daughter remained. And remained and remained (not really sanctioned). Past three cups of tea and snacks and into lunch and then after lunch. One thing she could count on was that she wasn't going to go hungry, as there was a steady stream of food to eat and to drink so that she was nourished and hydrated all day.

In the afternoon, she ventured into the library, which she quickly discovered was THE spot to be during exam study period. In fact, she realized that even had she arrived hours earlier, she might not have found the perfect place to sit. Just like visitors to a resort who are up at the crack of dawn to reserve a lounger by the pool, so too do students leave open text books to save their spot. Volunteers walked around with some sort of clicker, counting the number of occupied seats and taking note of those that were available. My daughter figured that the library was at 95 percent occupancy all day.

After putting in about seven hours of studying (she says that she's never studied like this before and I believe it), she wrote to say: "My brain hurts. Gonna take a break now and go back to studying tonight".

"Mom," she said, "you've got to write an article about how competitive it is to find a place to sit in the library during exam time."

She told me about how students in the know had come to the library with enough provisions so that they were fully equipped for the day. They only left when they had to—for bathroom breaks.

After her longer break and dinner, she met up with some friends who were also studying for the psychology exam. They introduced her to the world of studying in smaller groups in pre-reserved study rooms. There, they wrote notes to themselves and for one another on the blackboard and reviewed the material together. She found this incredibly helpful and a great social bonding experience, too. The same girls and she are planning on studying this way again the next night.

After working hard, they rewarded themselves by grabbing a coffee and chilling for a while together, before going to their rooms to try to get some shut-eye, so that they could wake somewhat replenished the following morning.

It seems to me that despite the hard work she is putting in, she is enjoying her first round of studying for exams at university (I actually told her, jokingly, that she was having way too much fun studying for exams).

DAY TWO OF STUDYING

My daughter called around 9:30 a.m. to say that she was up, but barely.

She showed me, over video, how she's been organizing her notes and I was impressed. Seems that the coloured pens really do motivate her, as everything was neatly written out in her notebook with colourful headings and lots underlined.

Studying doesn't come naturally to most students. Hopefully most will have picked up some tips from teachers in elementary and high school, but this is very different and I'm sure that along with what she is already putting into application, she will continue to learn as she advances from one set of exams to another.

As we await her arrival home next week, I'm stocking up on some Hanukkah gifts she requested on her wish list.

On that note, I wanted to mention how much she (and her fellow floormates) appear to love checking their personal mail boxes (like in an apartment building) and receiving mail or packages from home. Similar to being away at camp and receiving snail mail, there's something special about knowing that you've not been forgotten even after you've been gone for a while.

FIRST EXAM DAY

Last night, at midnight, after yet another evening of studying—this time with some of her floormates—she video called me from her room. She was furiously sharpening pencils and preparing herself for this morning, her first exam. The students have been drilled about the exam writing rules. For example, they are only allowed to bring specific bags with them in which to keep their coats, which are to be placed under their seats. No food is allowed. Water, preferably in clear bottles, is preferred.

She was eating wedges of orange she had cut up. "I'm getting a dose of vitamin C," she told me. Knowing that a good night's sleep and breakfast before her exam was a good idea (especially because, as she had studied, sleep helps to consolidate what you learn), she was hoping to go to sleep shortly after our conversation ended.

This morning, her dad and I called and texted good luck messages to her.

At around 8:15 a.m., she called to say that she was up and in the cafeteria.

"It's unreal in here," she told me.

In a cafeteria that is typically quite quiet this time of day, she said, it was swarmed with 1,500 psychology students all gobbling down breakfast while reviewing their notes one last time.

She sounded a little anxious, but ready for her first three-hour exam at university.

At around noon, which was the time the first exam was set to be over, I checked my Find A Friend App to see where my daughter was. I got a 'location not found' alert, meaning that her phone had likely been turned off, in accordance with the exam rules.

I was right because at around 12:30 p.m., when I checked again, I could see that she was somewhere close to her residence. I sent her a text asking how it had gone and she responded with "OK".

"OK?" I questioned.

"It was good," she responded back.

"OK," I said.

Since I have come to respect that, like most teens, she is not always eager to share details with me right after what I might consider a big event that I'm anxious to know more about, I told her to call when she was able to chat.

She called a couple of hours later and shared that despite the exam being scheduled to begin at 9 a.m., the 300 or so students (out of 1,500 in the same course) who were writing in that particular room, were left waiting in line outside the room for about a half hour, as officials weren't prepared for them to enter at that time. I can only imagine that for a mass of students, most writing their very first university exam, any amount of waiting was anxiety provoking.

Finally, they were ushered into the room so that each row of single desks and chairs were filled before students were pointed to the next row—I imagined this to look somewhat like the scene at a large parking lot where cars are directed towards the next empty space. Chairs and desks lined the entire huge room, even on the stage at the front of the room. My daughter found the enormity of the room and the number of students in it quite intimidating. As each entered the room, they were required to show their student ID cards and then to place the same card on the corner of their desk so that they could be identified, if needed, by the proctor supervising the students as they wrote their exam. Apparently, those who had misplaced or forgotten to bring their cards were fined $50.

The next day she was back with her nose to the grindstone. She was spending more time studying in her room, as opposed to the library, likely because she was feeling quite fatigued from the frustration of finding a seat. The university had announced that some exam de-stressor activities were taking place on the ground floor at various times. During the time specified, she joined some of her residence mates for snacks and an opportunity to pet and pamper pooches who were only too happy for the attention from adoring animal lovers. It has been found that stroking and being around animals can be very soothing and therapeutic at all times, but especially during times of stress.

The rest of the weekend was spent studying with floormates, working out at the gym and hanging out with other friends socially. All in all, she had a busy weekend leading up to another two exams, before she came home for a few days in between her third and fourth exams.

I'm sure that aside from wanting to see us and her friends back home, she's also looking forward to sleeping in. When I chatted with her last night via video, she looked half asleep. Our older daughter, sitting next to me as her sister and I chatted, suggested that she buy a Red Bull to keep her going. Her suggestion was meant to be a joke, because both girls know my views on that kind of antidote to tiredness. I've heard from my teenage clients attending university that there's a prevalence of students taking caffeine pills and other such stimulants, such as certain ADD medications (which act as a stimulant if you don't have ADD), which are not prescribed, but bought or given to them by others. (This confirmed what we learned at the parent presentation earlier in the year). Scary stuff.

My daughter assured me that even though she has "considered" trying one or the other, she hadn't. Call me naïve to believe that she was telling me the truth, but along with trusting her, I'm thinking that she wouldn't be looking so doggone tired if she had ...

The rest of the day was spent preparing for her third of four exams scheduled for the next day from 7 to 10 p.m. It surprises me that exams are scheduled for late in the evening, but perhaps I'm only thinking of how much less alert I would be at that time compared to in the morning. My daughter says that she doesn't mind it, as it gives her the entire day in which to study.

MID DECEMBER AND TAKING A BREAK

Now that my daughter has completed three of her four exams, and since there is a five-day break until the final one, she took the train home for some rest and relaxation, as well as studying time at home. On our way to picking her up, I began to think that as much as it must be amazing to come home to clean sheets and home-cooked meals, it must also be difficult to adjust not just to nagging parents, but also to not being able to step outside one's door and down the hall to hang out with any number of new friends, all with similar interests and issues. How coming back home must not only be warm and welcoming, but also somewhat lonely and boring by comparison.

She was in quite a chatty mood when we picked her up at the train station, and she continued to chat when we got home and had lunch together, and even throughout the day many of her sentences began with, "Oh, did I tell you about…?"

I learned all about the pranks pulled at university, including stealing trays from the cafeteria which double as toboggans, to be used goodness knows where (I guess wherever they can find a hill), the way in which the engineering students are traditionally not 'allowed' to touch their $500 jackets with their hands when they first get them, but instead 'slam' them all the way home, and then douse them in purple paint to 'break them in' before wearing them for the first time, after their exams in the fall.

The day after she arrived home, despite having the best of intentions to study for her cognitive science test scheduled for four days later, she was distracted by her friends who have begun trickling back into town for their Christmas Break. She and a high school friend even walked the hallowed halls of their old school in search of their favourite teachers.

Even though it's only been months since their graduation, I think that they're already feeling sentimental and nostalgic.

So, all in all, not much studying done so far, which reinforces my belief (and hers) that it's much easier to stay at university to study, rather than trying to do so at home.

Throughout her days back at home, she was quick to remind me of her ability to take care of and think for herself. At the same time, she was very willing and open to taking a break from caring for herself much of the time when it came to responsibilities such as doing laundry and making her own snacks.

"You know what happens mom," she said, after I suggested that she get a good night's sleep, "when parents stop reminding their kids to do things?" "What happens?" I asked.

"They begin to remind themselves."

I paused.

She was right.

But I apparently hadn't quite gotten it, because when I called from my office the following morning (after leaving her asleep in bed) to enquire as to whether she was up (she had an appointment to attend at noon) and then benignly asked if she had eaten breakfast, I got an impatient: "You do realize that I am capable of keeping track of things myself!"

I do recognize that she is capable and understand her need for increased autonomy, especially now that she has had a real taste of it, but old habits die hard.

Remembering that she doesn't need me to keep on top of her life is challenging for me, but liberating, too.

I've always been the kind of mom who acts like a meteorologist. I provide weather reports and even suggest what jacket to wear, whether or not to take an umbrella and which boots or shoes might be best.

Knowing that she has a warm winter coat and boots, along with gloves and toque, with her, allows me to at least know that she is well equipped for the cold. However, I have come to realize that I can't and should not be on top of everything. Not just because it requires more work on my part, but because it really doesn't give her the opportunity to think for herself. And isn't that part of why we send our kids off to university and college? To be better thinkers?

Remembering this is sometimes tough, especially when she FaceTimes me and her cheeks are burnt red from the wind chill, her hands are close to frost bitten and she tells me that she ran from the gym in a spring jacket and three-quarter length pants. I try to offer a sympathetic response, but no admonishment for not having dressed properly, hoping that the natural consequence of being cold will help her learn for next time.

MEETING THE LANDLORD

The reason that we drove my daughter from home and back to university to write her final exam (before heading home the same day for her Christmas Break) was so that we could meet her landlord and see the house in which she will be living, before she officially signs the lease.

Yes, she arranged this meeting and agreed that seeing her room may be a good idea, after all.

After reading through her lease, we had a list of questions we wanted to ask and a list of what we wanted to make sure was already in place, such as:

- Were the smoke alarms in proper working order and were there carbon monoxide detectors in place, too? Were they hard wired into the ceiling or did they need to have their batteries replaced at regular intervals?

- Was there a fire escape route figured out, especially for the students on the higher floors?

- What appliances came with the house and what kind of working order were they in? We planned on turning them on and off ourselves, too.

- What utilities were the girls responsible for, such as heat, water and gas? Also, was the water heater rented or owned by the landlord, and was the furnace gas or oil fueled? It apparently costs more to run a furnace with oil.

- When was the furnace and humidifier last serviced and what frequency of service could they expect in the future?

- How many gallons of water did the hot water tank hold? We also wanted to check the water pressure by turning on the shower and taps in the bathrooms and kitchen.

- We were advised to check out the electrical panel to see if it had fuses or breakers and to enquire how many amps it could sustain. We were told that 60 is the amperage for many homes, but ideally 100 would best suit a home with many tenants.

- Was there any exposed asbestos in the basement? This apparently looks like grey drywall.

- We presumed that the house would not come with central vacuum and that the girls would have to equip the home with a vacuum and cleaning supplies. And that they were responsible for bringing in all of their own furniture and equipment including kitchen supplies and microwave. But we wanted to make sure.

- Was there a cable outlet already hooked up (that is if they even want a TV since most teens, it seems, watch shows on their laptops) or whether this would be an extra cost?

- Also, was there internet and WiFi connection?

- Who would be responsible for driveway and walkway shovelling during the winter months?

- Was there any kind of housekeeping service for common areas or were the girls responsible for maintaining more than their bedrooms?

- Were the students the only ones signing the rental agreement or were we doing so as well?

- We wanted to check out the windows and to open and close them to make sure that they were in good working condition. Also, to find out if there were any window coverings provided or if the girls would be responsible for this.

- How often would garbage be collected and where it had to be placed for pick up and when? Also, if blue and green bins were provided to pick up recyclable waste.

- We wanted to enquire about security such as the effectiveness of locks on doors and windows. Also, whether the girls were allowed to install locks on their bedroom doors (if they didn't have them already).

- How monthly payments were to be made (i.e. via what method), and on what date? If he wanted a security deposit and if so, how much and to cover what?

- How much notice the landlord needs to give the tenants prior to showing up for any good reason? Who this notice is given to and via what method?

- Were there any prior issues with infestation of ants, rats, bed-bugs or cockroaches, for example? And if so, how the situation was dealt with and when?

- Of course, we also wanted to be able to check out the room that my daughter had been assigned and to consider which furniture would be able to fit in it (we figured we'd come back for measurements at a later date).

- And if something broke down, who the girls would contact and how soon they would be responded to?

- We were curious to know if each girl would have her own lease or if all of their names would appear on one. Further to this, what responsibility they would assume if one of the housemates left suddenly or planned to move out?

The hard part, I know, about asking so many questions, is developing enough of a good rapport with the landlord first, so that most are asked casually during a tour of the house, rather than appearing nitpicky or interrogative. As much as I know that we are entitled to answers to all of these questions, I don't want to begin the relationship with my daughter's future landlord on a negative note or get his back up. So, my plan is to make sure that at least the issues around safety and health are addressed first and then, depending on how things are going, ask the less important questions (and ones that are not deal breakers) last or another time.

We arrived at the home that she will be sharing with her four housemates next year. At first glance, both the street, with garbage cans and recycling containers strewn in front of the homes, seemed mostly run down and tired looking. Perhaps this had something to do with the grey skies and the dirty snow beneath our feet. One could immediately tell that this was student housing at its best—with students coming in and out of doors and walking along the street. Also, many of the homes were in various stages of renovation, mostly due to being run down for many years.

Although her future housemates had warned her (and she us) about the derelict state of the home, we were still somewhat surprised just how badly in need of a facelift it was.

We arrived at 2 p.m., the time that had been agreed upon. As we waited, my daughter checked her phone and exclaimed upon seeing an email that the landlord had sent the day before, but that she had not seen. He wrote to confirm today's meeting, but said he would consider it cancelled if he did not hear back with a confirmation on her end. We were very disappointed, having planned our trip around this meeting and armed with our list of questions waiting to be answered.

She called and fortunately reached him and he agreed to meet us 45 minutes later, after apologizing for the inconvenience, but explained that this was standard practice for their company, since they are typically stood up 30 percent of the time, and so don't want to waste their time showing up when a third of prospective tenants don't.

We were just glad to be let in.

Realizing that we were not going to be enthralled with the general state and structure of the house (aside from what appeared to be dirt that hadn't been cleaned in a while), he began by telling us about all the renovations that were planned prior to the girls July 1 occupancy date.

I had imagined that we would be with the landlord for about an hour—so that we could ask him some questions, but after 15 minutes he was already putting on his boots and tying his laces in an effort to get us out. He even looked at his watch once or twice before telling us he had to run.

In the end, I was only able to get the answers to a few of my questions. I realized, however, that students (and parents) are at the landlord's mercy since houses close to campus are in high demand and even those that are smaller and not in great condition will get grabbed quickly.

My daughter had plans to study with one of her floormates for her final exam of her first semester the next day and I had come prepared with my rubber gloves so that I could refresh her room and replace her bed linens.

I'm sure that the Don or whoever inspects the rooms to make sure that everything is unplugged and that windows are locked after all the students have left, will be impressed by the state she left her room in. My daughter says that she has heard that along with making sure that everything is sealed and secure, they are looking for items that the students are not supposed to have—toasters, candles, lighters and booze, for example.

She's not sure how deeply they really search for these forbidden items.

On the third day that she was home, I was invited to be a guest on another radio talk show. The host wanted me to comment on how to make the best of university and college students' time back home. He had found an article in which I had been quoted on this topic about a year prior, but this time I was, of course, talking from personal experience, too. Before the interview, I mentioned the topic to my daughter.

She said that at this point in time, she didn't feel that she needed nearly as much time to adjust as earlier on in the year. She also felt that nothing much changed for her when she parachuted back into our lives.

I, on the other hand, feel that we accommodate, and make changes whenever my daughter returns home, especially for longer visits.

- For example, on her return home in between exams, we stayed out of the living room (where we typically watch TV) so that she could study at the dining room table (adjacent to that room) for prolonged periods of time. Yes, we could have said she had to find another spot in which to study, but we figured it wasn't a huge concession for a short period of time.
- I put up with her "borrowing" my stuff, because she hadn't brought hers back home (my hair brush, for example).
- I've been reminded that teens typically live by a spontaneous time clock and that it's not always a given that they will know if they are joining you for dinner, even though its 5:30 p.m.

and you're beginning dinner prep. I've also been reminded that even if they haven't let you know that they will be joining you until 6:30 p.m., that they might complain about what you've made because surely you know that they prefer not to eat fish!

- We make sure to buy what she wants and have the items in the fridge upon her return (along with our usual provisions). We once even went in search of a specific type of noodle that are hard to find, because she really wanted to try them, bought spring mix in place of our usual lettuce (because she says it is more nutritious and she may be right) and snap peas because she likes crunch in her salad. And despite this, she called Uber Eats one evening to deliver chicken kebabs from a local Greek restaurant, because she had a craving for them.

- I am having to re-adjust not just the thermostat, but my internal thermometer to tolerate the heat on a higher temperature when she is home (actually, we've compromised by making it warmer during the day but cooler at night).

- I'm having to turn the dial of the radio in the bathroom back to my go-to station after she's changed it to hers when showering.

- It's become more and more clear that any attempt to organize or to discuss details for an upcoming outing for the family is typically perceived by her as me being controlling rather than organized or prepared.

- I stay awake way later than usual on the nights that she's out, because I prefer knowing that she's home safe before going to sleep.

- I have to put on my suit of protective armour to shield myself from some of her comments, which I try not to be overly sensitive about, but are still sometimes hurtful. Comments such as "why would you stop to speak to those people? You're so embarrassing" and "what is that perfume you're wearing?"

Today is December 21. The final day of exam writing for students at the university my daughter is attending. On Twitter, the university wrote that as of 5 p.m. today, approximately 18,407 (why do they say approximately and then come up with an exact number like that?) students will have written 64,061 exams between December 7 and today. Staggering numbers!

After exams were over, and she came home for a longer break, the first thing she did was to lie on the couch, cover herself with a blanket and stare at her cell phone for hours. As a parent, I've gotten used to her spending more time on her own or with friends than with us. After dinner, she organized her room (I convinced her to hang her clothes up rather than living from a suitcase since she would be with us for a longer period of time). At around 10 p.m. she came bouncing down the stairs with car keys in hand.

"Where you going?" I asked.

"Nowhere," she said. "I'm just putting my keys on the hook."

Then...

"And I'm about to make muffins."

Seriously? I thought, but said nothing.

What I wanted to say was that I was used to closing the kitchen, counters nicely wiped and sink cleaned, after dinner. Besides the odd plate being placed in the sink "after hours," I really didn't want to worry about it getting dirty again.

I didn't want to say anything though, because I realized that it would not only stunt her creativity, her initiative to try a new recipe for pumpkin muffins and do something other than looking at screens, but also because I didn't want her to think that keeping a clean kitchen was more important than all that.

Before I said anything, it was as if she read my mind (or maybe as a result of knowing me so well), because she said "I'm going to clean up".

"Go for it," I said.

Not that she was looking for my approval or permission, but I think she appreciated it as she bounced around the kitchen, opening and closing cupboards and whisking up the dry and then wet ingredients before placing the mixture in cupcake tins and putting them in the oven.

They were, in fact, delicious!

And she really did a good job cleaning up after, even according to my high standards.

What I came to know by the beginning of Christmas Break:

- To continue to grow my relationships with moms and parents of the kids that my daughter went through elementary and high school with, to share stories, support one another and nurture our friendships apart from our children.

- To keep informed about latest trends and behaviours amongst teens in regards to drug/alcohol use and sexual behaviour, so that I could be prepared for what I was hearing from her. I also continued to respond in a way that invited open communication and encouraged discussion/problem solving.

- To evaluate my internal response and monitor how I respond when communicating about safety practices. In other words, I tried to make sure that I was not making her feel that the world is an entirely unsafe place, while at the same time trying to make sure that she doesn't put herself in harm's way.

- To continue to encourage her to seek out resources on campus and to find ways to stay motivated and to take care of herself—physically and emotionally.

- To anticipate her return visits home with excitement, but also with greater awareness of how to manage them e.g. not to sweat the small stuff.

- To visit her as well as have her come home to us, so that we could be on her home turf and so that she could show us around more fully.

- To continue to pull back as she appeared less anxious and more settled, so that I could give her space to breathe and grow.

- To support her by being available when she needs me and by stepping in a little more when she is embarking on decisions that she has less life experience with, such as when she was signing a lease for a house.

- To continue to appreciate the benefits of not having to parent all the time, to not feel so heartsick when I walk past her bedroom with her not in it and to look forward to our conversations and texts.

CHAPTER ELEVEN

A FRESH START
FROM NEW YEAR'S ON

Happy New Year!

My daughter is anticipating the first week back to school with some trepidation. She says that it's called 'Frost Week', which I guess is in keeping with the below-zero temperature outside.

She's even suggested skipping the first week because apparently everyone is more focused on becoming inebriated rather than educated, but I've suggested that since she's never actually been at university during Frost Week before, that she at least attend this year to really know what she might have missed during the first of her classes in each new subject this semester. She didn't fight me on this, so I'm figuring that she realizes that there is likely some truth to my thinking. Turns out, had she not gone, she would have missed more than she thought.

Besides, the honeymoon is long over and I think her parent annoyance meter is registering way into the red zone by now. She has returned to her predictable pre-first year position—that of being in her bed devouring the latest series on Netflix.

Having spoken to many parents whose children have returned home over the last few weeks, and especially those who are in their first year of being away, I don't feel alone in thinking that familiarity can breed contempt and that yes, distance does make the heart grow fonder.

I also know that I'm not alone in realizing now that the fantasy of what having your teen back home will look like is often different than what actually transpires.

I am no longer under the illusion that we will spend our evenings playing board games around the dining room table when she visits.

I now know that along with coping with the disappointment of not feeling that we are the most important people in our teen's life, and the disappointment that everything very quickly falls back into a familiar dynamic, that coming to terms with this also means recognizing that a lot of our teen's behaviour has nothing to do with us. It is as a result of typical teenage responses to feeling that they are being controlled and managed a whole lot more than they have become comfortable with over the past couple of months, in particular.

Along with the emotional adjustment and coming to terms with reality, I've also heard from many parents about the practical and environmental adjustments that need to be realized. One mom told me that she's not used to so many extra shoes crowding the front entrance; another about how much more laundry there is to take care of, and how much more food is consumed, even with one extra person at home. I know I'm not alone when I talk about the changes to routine, to not being able to settle at night knowing that your teen is wanting to take the car out at 11 p.m. or have friends over when you have to get up for work in the morning.

With this all being said, there is something comforting about knowing that your teen is (for the most part), safely under your roof even though it really upsets you that they're staring at screens or staying up until 3 a.m. to complete an assignment that's due in the same day. Also, something rewarding about seeing the mature (or more mature) adult he or she is becoming and even reconnecting with their friends who you've known all their lives, too.

I woke up on the morning that my daughter was leaving again, with a pit in my stomach and a lump in my throat. I knew that saying goodbye would be bittersweet, because although we had bickered and locked horns on several occasions over the past few weeks, I knew that saying goodbye again would be hard.

She had been up late the night before, hanging out in our basement with about a dozen friends, the majority leaving that day to go back to university.

As a result of being up so late, it was difficult for her to wake up and it was only because of the delicious smell of bacon and eggs that her dad had prepared that motivated her to join us for breakfast at 10:30 a.m. It was time for her to get up because her friend's parents who were driving their daughter back to the same university, had kindly offered to pick her up at noon. This was a good thing, because aside from the clothing she had brought back with her (all neatly washed and dried and packed away), she had a couple of bags of groceries which included cereal, popcorn, fruit and yoghurt.

After breakfast, and once she had double checked that all was packed away, she slumped back on her bed and asked if I could massage her aching legs (she had spent too long and worked out too hard with her very fit cousin at the gym the day before). While watching her angelic face on the pillow, I massaged one leg and then the other. All the negative interactions from the previous weeks fell away and were replaced by bittersweet emotion. I tried not to get too caught up in examining the heel of her foot while reminding myself that it was the size of her whole foot as a baby. I didn't want to get swallowed up in nostalgia, so I pulled myself back to reality before it was time to say goodbye.

"I love you," I said, as I hugged her.

She hugged me back.

"I love you, too," she said.

About an hour into the drive back, I received a text from her sharing her innermost thoughts about feeling conflicted about returning to residence. On one hand, she was sad to leave her home and us, but on the other, she looked forward to being away from the daily nagging and arguments with us and her sister.

Still, despite feeling saddened by her internal conflict, I was glad that she was able to share this with me, perhaps so that we could explore this and try to make her next visit home, better.

This time, settling back into residence was even easier. She wasn't feeling anxious at all. Later, she stood in a long lineup outside the cafeteria for dinner. They were apparently only letting small groups of people in as others left. She said she hadn't seen it as crowded since she first moved into residence and wondered why. I suggested that it may have something to do with students returning to the cafeteria the night before their first day of their second semester, rather than exploring places further afield, as they may have become accustomed to doing as their last semester unfolded.

She called me once back in her room. "My room's an absolute mess," she said. "I've got to clean it." I said nothing, but her words were a reminder that despite not keeping her room at home as clean and neat as I like to keep the rest of the house, that when living alone, she feels more comfortable when she returns her space to a certain standard of living. Also, a reminder to me that her letting go when she's home for the weekend or even a couple of weeks (or months!) is likely either a regression to earlier days when she knew that I would come in and tidy for her (I don't anymore), or her desire to take a break from being so responsible when living away from home.

Fraternities and sororities may become a big part of one's social circle at university, if one chooses or is able to belong to one. Her boyfriend's fraternity, one of the many AEPi (Alpha Epsilon Pi) chapters from around the world, meets once a week in a room at the university, but it is apparently not officially affiliated with the university. Their parties are primarily held at a house that is rented exclusively by guys in the same fraternity and they fundraise by having other events (such as an all-ages party at a place in town) as they did during Frost Week.

When she and her boyfriend first arrived at the party, she was the only rose amongst the thorns, so to speak—the only female with 12 brothers, all of whom are a tight knit group of friends. She was cool with hanging out and watching them play beer pong and I think they were impressed that she let them do their thing without rolling her eyes or pouting. At the end of their game when they raised their (plastic) glasses in a toast "to the brothers" she piped in "and one sister". They laughed and said that she fit in just right. That made her feel good, too.

As other guys and girls arrived, and the more she had to drink, the more comfortable she became chatting with people, making new friends and enjoying the party in a way she had not anticipated.

Seeing the camaraderie amongst the brothers has inspired her to reconsider visiting the sorority she's heard about on campus. Maybe even to connect with other girls she knows about creating their own. Although not for everyone, being part of a fraternity or sorority may create a greater sense of belonging for students living away from home and an opportunity to broaden their social circle.

This semester, my daughter doesn't begin class until 12:30 p.m. on Mondays. However, I've encouraged (not told!) her to "consider" waking up earlier on this day, so that she can put time into her online course.

I am typically not that in favour of online courses (for clients or my own children) unless the student is incredibly motivated in general or has a huge interest in the course itself. Online courses require a great amount of not only motivation, but also self-discipline.

My daughter chose the pharmacology course, because she needed a fifth subject to complete her second semester and could not find any in-class subjects, other than what she had already chosen, that appealed to her. Pharmacology did.

Along with personal interest in the subject matter (their first assignment is on the pros and cons of marijuana use), I'm also hoping that when living in residence at university (as opposed to being a high school student living at home), that there will be an increased commitment to work towards obtaining the credit and doing well, especially because she is living in an academic environment. The proof will be in the pudding, so to speak.

It's mid January and she is attending class, socializing with her friends and boyfriend, volunteering at the crisis line, and assuming her other responsibilities.

Last night she called to ask if she could still eat cheese that has some mold growing on it. A peer had told her that cheese is supposed to grow mold and that the part that is not moldy can still be eaten. I asked if the mold was throughout the block or only on the edge and what the expiry date was.

After learning that it was still apparently good for another couple of weeks, I agreed that it was OK to cut off the moldy part and still eat what looked good, as long as it tasted good, too.

I've noticed that we are speaking a lot less these days. I've even noticed a decline in checking my tracking device to see where she is. So, there are many days when I suddenly realize that it's 3 p.m. and that we haven't had any contact since the night before. And even more shocking to me, that I haven't felt compelled to check her whereabouts.

I am settling into feeling more comfortable in knowing that she can take good care of herself, that she is living in a safe environment and that she is the kind of person who needs space to breathe and grow.

All in all, my daughter appears quite settled and relaxed about not seeing us for weeks at a time.

One evening she worked at the crisis line and then had a friend come over with chicken nuggets and a bottle of wine. Then, later that night, after things had quietened down a bit, someone got hold of a fire extinguisher and sprayed its contents into the air, setting off the fire alarms and creating havoc with fire engines and ambulances showing up within minutes. She, along with her residence peers, had to stand outside in the freezing cold hours of the morning for a half hour before authorities declared that the residence was safe to re-enter. Such is the life on residence…my daughter is looking so forward to not living there next year.

One night, after a difficult day, she called me at midnight.

She sounded agitated and wanted to know if, when she took the phone away from her ear and held it towards the ceiling, I too could hear the repetitive knocking sound. It was very faint from where I was listening, but when you're tired and emotional, and you have no control over the consistent knocking sound when you're trying to go to sleep, it can be extremely annoying.

Never mind annoying. It was driving her "f-ing crazy".

I wasn't sure what I could do to help, but suggested that she might want to try to reach the Don or a 24-hour physical plant emergency department if it continued. She didn't seem enthused by my suggestions, but what else could I do?

I lay awake for 15 minutes listening to my husband snoring and wondering what I could do to stop the noise in my bedroom, too (payback for the nights I've kept him awake with the same sound, I guess).

Before trying to go back to sleep, I texted her for an update and thankfully, the knocking had stopped.

Again, I am reminded of the push/pull that I experience with my daughter. She's independent, responsible, books her own appointments and has proven herself capable of so much, but when she feels like she's being driven crazy by a sound she can't stop, when her toe is hurting or when her body is not acting the way she knows it normally does, it's kind of nice to know that she still sees me as her go-to person.

I feel like we are human yo-yos. Sometimes it's my daughter with the string around her finger and sometimes it's around mine. Depending on who's executing the action, she's letting the yo-yo drop and then pulling it towards her, or vice versa. So, too, is the "don't leave, please go" tension we feel towards one another—especially as this first year away at university unravels.

One of the companies that has been sending me and my daughter emails about rental opportunities over the past few months, sent one last email indicating that all of their properties have been rented for the following school year. Not to say that this is the same for every rental agency or landlord, but at this point in time, if a student hasn't organized housing for the next school year, they are definitely falling behind.

"I can't feel my feet," she told me, in the same tone as if she was telling me she had just gotten out of bed and was on her way to breakfast.

"You can't what?" I asked, not sure I had heard her correctly the first time.

"I can't feel my feet," she repeated. "They feel like they have pins and needles and I can't walk on them."

Had she not told me about the high-heeled shoes she had danced in at the party the night before, in addition to then walking to her boyfriend's house, I might have suggested she go to an emergency department right away.

I asked if they were swollen. No. So I suggested that she walk on them with comfortable shoes, despite the discomfort, to get her circulation moving and that she see a doctor if the pain or numbness got worse. What I really wanted to suggest was that she dump the ridiculously high-heeled shoes in the garbage, but I didn't because I figured that the numbness she was experiencing might be bad enough to discourage her from wearing them again.

She also shared that she felt ill from too much booze shortly after she arrived at the party. As I have learned to do, and especially because I know that she knows what's best for her, even though she doesn't always listen to what she knows, I didn't berate her for irresponsible drinking, but instead commented on how that must have put a dampener on the rest of her evening.

With only about five hours sleep, she was surprisingly chatty and sharing details, for which I was grateful. During our conversation, she revealed that she didn't know how she felt about her night out or about having to drink copious amounts in order to relax enough, in her estimation, to have a good time. I was relieved that she wanted to talk to me about this, and so I gave her my full attention.

Later, she filled me in on the details of her day.

She had taken a nap after lunch despite her good intentions to restructure her essay, due in at 11:59 p.m. that evening, and shared how disappointed she was in herself. I told her that, with about seven hours to go before midnight, she might be more productive now that she'd napped, than if she'd struggled through it with little sleep. Not that I want to condone sleeping during the day or staying out late on the day an essay is due, but I meant what I said and it seemed to make her feel better, too.

She informed me that she had heard back from a couple of places to which she had applied for summer work. I'm glad that she's applying now through various online sites, so that she can figure out plans for the months that she will be home.

That evening, knowing that her boyfriend was busy acting as bouncer at his frat brothers' party house, she connected with some female friends on her residence floor before all of them headed out to the same by-invitation-only party. Since her group of friends had not been officially invited, she wasn't sure if they would be allowed entry, but she figured she had some clout with the bouncer…and she was right.

They joined the wall-to-wall throngs of people (she said that it felt like there were hundreds of people inside).

"Once you got in, it was hard to get out," she told me. Reminded me of the Hotel California song, I told her.

Unfortunately, with so little space between one body and another, one of her friends was "groped" by someone she didn't know and then wanted to leave. Wanting to support her friend and recognizing that so many people might lead to even more trouble (to say nothing of the numbers being in violation of fire codes), my daughter and her friends were preparing to leave when everyone was asked to do so.

At first, she didn't know why an evacuation had been announced. Then, she noticed, as many made their way outside, (not everyone was willing or sober enough to do so) that there was a guy passed out in the front of the house. Her boyfriend told her that campus security had been alerted and that an ambulance was on its way. Knowing that they would be asked to shut down the party with that many people inside the house, the request for everyone to leave had been made.

The following day, perhaps as a result of how ill she felt when drinking too much a few nights before, along with her experience at the frat party the previous night, she informed me that she had changed her mind and instead of sticking around for the St. Patrick's Day party weekend, she wanted to come home after all. She confessed that despite initially wanting to be part of the hype, she really wasn't inclined towards the level of partying that would be happening the entire weekend. In particular, she declared that she wasn't into "day drinking," which as the name implies, is apparently how everyone spends their days (and nights) on weekends such as this. I supported her decision and was glad that she had made it on her own, without any pressure from me.

Apparently, the city in which my daughter is living has voted unanimously to pass a nuisance party bylaw, which means that if people (students) throw parties that create excessive noise or where there is public intoxication—especially outside on streets or the sidewalk—that fines of between $500 and $10,000 will be imposed.

Although it wasn't in time for the St. Patty's parties, it took effect shortly shortly thereafter. Many university towns and cities have passed similar bylaws.

Time is marching by quickly and my daughter is gearing up to begin studying for her end-of-year exams, which begin mid-March, which is in a couple of weeks. At the same time, she is trying to wrap her head around what career she sees herself in after university, which goes in hand with which programs she chooses to major and minor in, if she so chooses, next year. Her appointment with an academic advisor (yes, she finally did see one) revealed that she would likely benefit more from speaking to a career counsellor, so she made an appointment for that as well.

In the end, I have to trust that my daughter will find the answers she is looking for and that I will continue to guide her as much as she will allow me.

Choosing a career in one's first year of university really isn't easy, especially when there are so many years of learning and growing to come.

At around 4:30 p.m., I texted my daughter to call me after the meeting to let me know what she's doing with the rest of her life.

At around 5 p.m. she called. At first it sounded as if she was crying, but then I realized that her voice sounded as it did because she was feeling so incredibly joyful.

"OMG," she said, "the counsellor was so amazing. It was like an instant connection."

She suggested that my daughter purchase a book titled *Do What You Are: Discover the Perfect Career for You Through the Secrets of Personality Type,* by Paul and Kelly Tieger and Barbara Barron.

As a parent, I'm so thrilled that she continues to carve out relationships with wonderful mentors and supports while away from home and that universities offer these services that would otherwise be quite costly, to students who want (or need) them.

HOME—AGAIN

She commented on how it seems that every time she returns home for the weekend, we spend at least some of the time at a mall (and my credit card sees a surge in spending activity). This is apparently not an uncommon theme for parents and their teens in from university or college for bursts of time. There's typically a list of items to purchase (you'd think that their residences were in some remote area away from modern conveniences)—anything from a new toothbrush, underarm deodorant or socks.

This time, her mission was to find a new little black dress to wear to her boyfriend's end-of-year fraternity formal the following weekend. Fortunately, we found what she wanted in the third store and only two hours into our expedition.

On the way back to the train station I asked my daughter if she was as ready to leave residence as she expected to be. From her response, it sounds as if, now that the year is coming to an end, that she is feeling a host of bittersweet emotions. She shared her experience a few nights before coming home when 16 of the girls on her floor all happened to be using the bathroom at the same time and how, despite having to share a handful of sinks and the space being somewhat cramped, it had been fun to all share in the experience of brushing their teeth and performing their evening rituals together.

It sounds as if, even though they haven't all spent intense periods of time together over the year, that being in the same boat, learning how to share and be tolerant, developing patience and persistence, has created a bond between them. Now, despite thinking that she would be only too glad to move on and out of residence, she is already feeling nostalgic and hoping that there will be some sort of closing ritual before they say good-bye and spread out in different directions for the summer, not knowing how often their paths will cross when they return to their new homes in September, ready to begin their second year with renewed energy and enthusiasm (hopefully!).

I am anticipating my daughter's semi-permanent return home from university in less than a month. I worry about how we are going to manage to navigate our way around one another for four months. I so strongly desire to make the most of our time together, to be the type of laid back, go-with-the-flow mom who is able to ignore a less-than-perfect environment and just appreciate having her home, but that's easier said than done.

Today is April 6 and the last day of the first year at university for my daughter.

Come to think of it, I hadn't checked the tracker for a while—in fact, I couldn't even remember where I last left it.

And knowing this made me realize that change, no matter how slow, had been happening. She and I were both navigating the world more independently. She is making mature, adult decisions and showing a great deal of success with the choices she is making and I am giving her more room in which to make them.

Over the past week, we have received emails from the university reminding us about the move-out process and the importance of leaving residence within 24 hours following her final exam, unless prior permission to stay had been granted. We've been told about returning room keys and where, or a financial penalty would be incurred, the state in which the rooms are to be left, along with the importance of making sure that everything has been removed, and the consequences for not doing so.

I'm tired of reminding my daughter about the importance of getting proper measurements of her room at the new house before we begin looking at furniture to fill it. I've decided that if she doesn't find a way to make this happen, then she will have to deal with the consequences of not knowing what will fit. Not me.

Apparently, she and her future housemates found the perfect sectional couch for their tiny living room. It's compact and just the right colour. The seller had bought it for $800, but was willing to let it go for $300. The girls were excited until they heard that someone else had put in an even higher bid than the $350 they ultimately agreed to pay (the seller upped the price when she realized it was such a hot commodity) and then they lost it to a group of students who agreed to pay $600 dollars for it!

Tonight, she complained about having to do laundry when other people were out partying. Laundry and studying. Not a winning combination, but I reminded her that it might be the last time she has to use the residence laundry facilities before the year is done.

"I guess I have no choice," she said. "I'm running out of underwear."

"Well, you could always wear them inside out," I said jokingly.

"That's gross," she exclaimed. "Why can't I just order some new ones online?"

"Are you being serious?" I asked.

"Yes, I need new ones anyway."

"Well, we can deal with that when you return," I said. "For now, just wash what you have."

I've heard from a few friends whose teens are in the process of studying and writing exams now too, that some have returned home for a few days of TLC while studying. Some are nursing colds and sore throats. My daughter is complaining about chronic heartburn and indigestion and asking for my advice about what she can do about it.

I've heard that some of the symptoms she's describing may be related to stress, too, or may be as a result of the handfuls of veggie chips she may be idly consuming in the library as she reads through and tries to memorize her notes.

In the midst of her studying, she's continuing to try to find a summer job and to figure out what she's going to do with the rest of her life.

I've tried to guide her towards not piling her plate so high right now. Tried to convince her that studying and getting good results on her exams should be her priority, but it's not easy to stay focused on just that when she feels as if there are so many loose ends to tie up in a very short amount of time.

Last night, she called me at 10:30 p.m. to say that she was going to try to sleep earlier than usual.

"Without melatonin tonight," she told me.

"Why?" I asked.

"Because I think I've become too dependent on it to get to sleep. I just need to get to bed earlier."

I was glad to hear that.

When I woke up this morning shortly after 7 a.m., I saw that a text had come in from her at 6:43 a.m.

"You up?" she wrote.

"I am now," I wrote back.

She called.

"I'm so anxious," she shared. "Exam anxiety is different to other anxieties," she said. "It woke me out of my sleep this morning. I have diarrhea, my palms are sweaty and I feel hyper inside." I told her that there was a good cure for that.

"What now, doc?" she asked sarcastically.

"Write the exam," I responded.

The best cure for anticipatory anxiety is to do what you're afraid of. It's almost never as anxiety producing as you think it will be. Even though this is not the first exam my daughter has written, she says that the anxiety is the same each time.

In addition to typical anticipatory anxiety, a lot was riding on this psychology exam. She's wanting an automatic acceptance into the competitive psychology stream in second year. She figured out that she needed a 69 on her exam in order to score an A minus, which is what is required for this to happen.

At the end of the year, she did achieve high enough grades to be given an automatic acceptance into the psychology stream of her bachelor's program, which she was thrilled about.

CHAPTER TWELVE

CHANGING DIRECTION: PACKING UP

With some coaching along the way, my daughter became less anxious after each exam, which brought her closer to the end of first year and to returning "home" for the summer months.

It is hard to believe that in just five days, there will be a trailer hitched to our car and we will be heading towards helping her pack up and leave residence.

I am feeling a surge of nervous energy, similar to what I had experienced before she left. I re-organized the entire basement, threw away and gave away items I'd been storing forever, and organized the piles of paper that I'd been meaning to get to. I think in some way I was getting myself prepared again. Trying to create some order and calm in preparation for her return.

So here we are. Spending another overnight (never factored this into the cost of university!) in the city in which my daughter has lived for the past eight months. We got hitched at U-Haul yesterday and went back this morning to have the 5 X 8-foot trailer attached to the back of my car. By the time all was said and done, we were on the road by around 10:30 a.m. and with a few stops for coffee, washroom breaks and more gas, we arrived in time to find our daughter walking towards her residence, after meeting with her TA regarding an assignment on which she had asked for verbal feedback.

But before we arrived, I received a series of texts.

"By the way," she said, "do I have to wash my dishes? Or can I bring them home dirty?"

I laughed at what I first considered a rhetorical question.

"By dirty, do you mean that they have food on them?"

Pause.

"Yeah."

"Well, then, I suggest you give them at least a good rinse."

I was already dreading dragging home so much. I hadn't considered that there might be food-encrusted plates thrown into the mix, too.

Before we even entered her room, my daughter offered to treat us to lunch. Well, technically I guess we were treating ourselves to a few of her unused TAMs—or Trade A Meal—which were part of her meal plan. With almost 50 TAMs still unused, and knowing that she has to forfeit whatever is remaining, now that she has completed her year in residence, she's trying to gobble up whatever she can. The whole meal plan thing is like a foreign language to me, so I just trust that she knows what she's doing.

After refuelling our bodies, we set out to tackle her room. It wasn't terribly disheveled, especially considering that she had been studying and writing exams for the past week or so, but those familiar dust bunnies were definitely as abundant as anticipated. Fortunately, I had dragged a plastic bucket, more rags and cleaning solution up to her room (much to her embarrassment) so that I could wipe the large storage containers (she thinks I'm totally nuts to do so), but I'd rather leave as much of the dust behind as I can. The white rug in the middle of her floor (which is now a dark grey) was carefully folded into a garbage bag and tightly sealed. I'm hoping it will fit into our washing machine.

I had forgotten just how much stuff we had lugged into her room when she moved in. Today I was reminded of it. Not only were there large items such as the fridge and mattress topper, but it's all the knickknacks that make the packing process seem never ending. Just when you think you're ready to close up one box, so she discovered another drawer full of bits and pieces, many that she hadn't even opened or used.

"I swear that I am going for the minimalist look next year," she said.

"I'm hoping that you'll remember that," I responded.

"I can't bear the thought of doing this at the end of every year," she said. "I'm hoping that I get along with my housemates well enough that I won't want to move until I graduate."

"Me too," I said.

Part way through the packing process, I went to the washroom to clean the rag I was using. The shower that never turns off was still running. I moved from the sink that had strands of pasta circulating above the plug to another that was less offensive. Above the sinks, on the ledge, were plates that were air drying.

Why, I wondered, do they not have a laundry type sink so that the students can at least wash the plates they use in their bedrooms?

Once we had packed up almost all of the room's contents, taken posters and decorations off the walls, taken expired items out of the fridge and even vacuumed all the dust bunnies from under her bed, we went for dinner with my daughter and her boyfriend and then back to the hotel to relax before loading all of the contents into the trailer the following morning.

We were glad to be staying overnight so as to take a breather rather than deal with the exhaustion of packing and unpacking all in one day.

We invited our daughter to join us overnight, thinking that she might look forward to a quieter night and more comfortable bed, but she said she'd prefer to spend one more night in residence.

"My only regret is not getting to know as many people on my floor as I could have," she said, after borrowing and returning a roll of duct tape to a fellow resident she didn't know so well.

Turns out that living in residence wasn't so bad an experience after all.

And so here I stand—on the precipice of a four-month period of living together again. My feelings are mixed.

It is truly hard to believe that so many months have passed since dropping her off. We were in a similar looking hotel room back then. I was so anxious about saying goodbye. About her living away from home and about missing her terribly. And now, ironically, I am feeling anxious about her coming home.

I worry about us navigating our lives around one another. I'm nervous about saying the wrong thing, completely unintentionally. I worry about her resistance, her reactivity, her irreverence. I worry about having to justify my actions towards her sister so as to ward off sibling rivalry, worry that the improved relationship we've experienced over the months will not continue when we're living in the same space.

Packing up the room and then the trailer was about as stressful as anticipated. I'm really glad that we packed, then stayed overnight, then loaded everything into the trailer the following morning, because had we done it all in the same stretch, tempers would have flared more quickly. As it was, we argued about whether or not it was worthwhile co-ordinating use of the elevator. Even though my daughter was only two flights up, I thought that it made a lot more sense to load the elevator a few times rather than lugging boxes and containers and even the fridge down the hall, stairs and into the trailer. My daughter insisted that she alone could do the lugging if we wanted her to, and her dad, wanting to prove to his daughter that he is still young and virile, went along with her plan.

Ultimately, a kind caretaker who had known my daughter over the year, offered to assist them by taking some of the boxes and the fridge into the elevator and thankfully, they agreed.

Word of caution: unplug the fridge/freezer 24 hours in advance of moving it, and then before doing so, open the fridge armed with paper towel or rags to mop up the flood of water that will escape as you open the door. Even then, depending on the vehicle in which you will be transporting it, have blankets to place under it so that the water can be absorbed along the way if more seeps out.

During the process of arguing as to whether an elevator was necessary or not, my daughter was triggered by something I said (can't even remember what) and after hours of helping her sort, pack and load, I too was triggered and told her "if I have to watch everything that comes out of my mouth, I just won't speak to you at all".

"Fine by me," she retorted and left the room with another box, leaving me with my thoughts and a few boxes yet to be taken down.

Perhaps she thought a little more about it on her way down. Perhaps she just didn't want to escalate the tension. Perhaps she realized that the stress of moving out might have influenced her reaction.

Whatever the reason, when she returned for another box, she spoke to me as if nothing had happened. And I, not wanting to make the situation more stressful, took her lead.

Once the last item had been removed, we stood in the hallway as she closed the door to a room she had learned to see as a safe and happy place. I purposely stood a few steps back, wanting to give her the space to say goodbye. To bring closure to her first year away from home.

At first, she closed the door and went to lock it as she had done hundreds of times since last September, but then she said out loud what she must have been thinking in her head:

"No, wait," and she opened the door again.

And stood there for about 30 seconds, looking into the room from the hallway, as if silently meditating and breathing the image of her room in for one last time.

Then, as my husband waited in the car, she and I walked a block away to pick up some more food (and to make use of more TAMs) for the road.

Moving out was so much easier than moving in. Not just because there's less of an emotional pulling at your heart, but because everyone is leaving on different days and different times, depending on when they write their final exam, so there's a lot less traffic and people congestion to deal with.

What I came to know during the second part of first year:

- To encourage my daughter to make decisions with confidence and to learn from her mistakes.
- To prepare myself for more of a hustle and bustle time and a greater dent in my wallet when she was in town.
- To recognize the shift in family dynamics and continue to navigate them better.
- To continue to help guide her through academic and social challenges.
- To try to remain sensitive to the transition that we are all a part of.
- I was able to see both sides—positive and negative—to living with grown children and coming to terms with letting go.

SECTION FOUR

MOVING BACK HOME

CHAPTER THIRTEEN

RETURNING TO THE NEST

After not getting much sleep the night before (she had stayed up into the early hours of the morning with people she had gotten to know well, in addition to some she wanted to know better while she had the chance), and the stress of moving, I should have known better than to be baited into conversation that sparked controversy while driving home.

However, there we were arguing about whether she should be allowed to have a lock on her bedroom door and why she can't just come and go without checking with us first, and why we need to figure out who's doing laundry and when, so that we don't step on each other's toes.

I knew not to expect too much excitement about returning home. I tried not to take it personally. I reminded myself that living on campus means that one doesn't have to go far to find a friend, means living in a close-knit community where everyone is a similar age, in sync with each other (at least academically) and speaks the same language, so to speak. I reminded myself about how bittersweet it must feel to return home where rules, restrictions and routine prevail.

I realize that the benefit of living on one's own is that you can be your own boss. If you don't want to eat dinner at 6:30 p.m. when "dinner's on the table" is announced, you don't have to. If you want to leave your clothes in a pile on the floor (even after you've just washed them), there's no one nagging you to hang them in your closet. No one nagging you to go to sleep. If you don't feel like talking, you can close your door and not come out until you want to or let voice mail capture the incoming call on your cell phone.

It appears that she would trade the home-cooked meals, the private shower and snuggling with her cats (well, maybe not!) for the chance to live alone. And maybe this is a good thing, because if the opposite were true, I might not be as OK with her living away from home.

But there's an art to living with others. An art to letting others know when you want to be left alone. An art to skillfully navigating around each other—in the living room, the kitchen, the bathroom. Even the laundry room.

I attempted to share this awareness with her.

I mentioned how well she had mastered the art of living alone, how even more of an independent thinker and doer she had become. I suggested that learning to live in close proximity with others is even harder to do. "I can live with others just fine, if they're not telling me what to do!" she retorted.

I was triggered by this. I tried to maintain my cool when talking to her about the difference between a parent telling her teen what to do versus negotiating a system and routine that is mutually respectful of everyone's needs.

"It's important that we are mutually respectful if we want to live peacefully in the same house for the next four months."

I said nothing more, because she was silent after that. One of the things I've learned is not to fill the silence that often represents the wheels turning in her head. I've come to realize that if I interrupt the flow of thoughts that might bring about heightened awareness, that I may push her, instead, in a different direction.

And as we pulled into our driveway, so did our neighbour pull into his.

"Hi," he said to her. "Long time no see. How's it been?"

"It's a journey," she replied.

CONCLUSION
IT'S A JOURNEY!

As I put the finishing touches on *Don't Leave, Please Go*, my daughter has almost completed her second year. We survived last summer's break together, this academic year has gone by even faster than the first and we have both continued to learn and grow. She is loving living in a house with four other girls who have surpassed her expectations of what ideal housemates would be. She is enjoying her independence and is a whiz at doing laundry—her own way!

Although she loves to experiment with different ingredients in the kitchen, she was finding it hard to keep up with shopping and chopping and cooking from scratch. Since her housemate told her that she was ordering from one of the meal-in-a-box companies, (they provide door-to-door delivery of fresh ingredients on a weekly basis, based on your choice of recipes), she's been doing the same. Now she's in competition with her dad when posting the best-looking food creations online and she's developing a repertoire of signature dishes. I haven't even heard anything about her feeling anxious in a long time.

As a parent I continue to feel us pushing and pulling at times, but I have learned that as hard as it is to pull back and let go, I have become so much better at it.

I've also learned to trust that the world is not going to gobble her up, but that it is more likely to embrace her as she carves out new paths and overcomes obstacles. I've realized that when I step back and wait, she amazes me with what she already knows, how she interacts with others and negotiates her way in the world.

I continue to be available to help her problem solve (without giving her the solution), to listen to her by validating and acknowledging (rather than giving unsolicited advice), and to believe that she can accomplish anything she sets her mind to achieve, no matter how challenging it is along the way.

Most of all, I've learned that learning how to live apart and then how to live together, while difficult at times, is part of the dance that ultimately allows each of us to realize true inner strength and the power within and between us.

By the end of first year, you will likely find that you have forged a healthier, better relationship by not living with your teen all the time and that this is just the beginning of a lifelong journey towards finding a good balance between holding on and letting go—of one another!

FINAL WORDS FROM MY DAUGHTER, CHLOE...

HOW FIRST YEAR SHOT ME DOWN, AND HOW I KEPT ON GOING

"Really? I would've never known…" is the recent response I got from a friend who just found out how really hard first year was for me. I guess that's exactly it. You wouldn't be able to tell just from looking at me.

My first year at university was not an easy one, to say the least. I expected it to be difficult. I realized that it would be harder, because I'd never been away to summer camp, like many others had, and I tried to assure myself that it was OK if I felt upset for the first little while.

After the first few weeks of school had passed, and it was the first week of October, Homecoming was on the minds of students. Halloween costumes were being made or bought, and I was still feeling upset. I thought the adjustment period would be over by then. This sadness turned into panic.

Why haven't I made good friends yet? Who am I going to go to

Homecoming with? What if I don't have someone to eat dinner with tomorrow?

These were some of the thoughts that constantly ran through my mind. And as the time passed, the more I worried. I told myself I would make friends in class, but when I didn't, I worried some more. I told myself I would join clubs and make friends, but I didn't.

That's when I sought help. I started seeing a counsellor to talk about these thoughts that constantly filled my head. And it helped for the hour I was with him, but then they came back. I went back to my room where again, I felt alone and worried about the future. I became so worried about the future that I couldn't focus on the present. It started taking over my life, affecting my ability to sleep and do work properly.

When I went home for the winter break, it was difficult to come back to campus. And so was every time I had to come back from home. Knowing what I was coming back to was always hard, but yet I still kept coming back. Why?

See, I've been asked this question recently…If you were having such a bad time, why didn't you leave? Why didn't you throw in the towel if it was making you that unhappy?

Well, the truth is, I don't really know. Thinking back, I'm not sure what kept me going. Maybe it was because I knew that if I came home, I might feel even worse. I had looked so forward to going away and attending my first choice of university and I didn't want to let myself down and have regrets when I looked back. I also had great support at home and parents who kept reminding me that it was important to keep going. I was continuing to see a counsellor and it was helping more.

By the time first semester came to a close, I gave myself a pat on the back. I felt proud of myself. I felt that staying was a huge accomplishment. I felt that I had overcome one of the most difficult times of my university experience. I reminded myself that it can and will get better. Yes, you need to do what makes you happy, but at the same time, the hardships you experience will teach you more about yourself than you'll ever know. Now that I'm almost at the end of my second year, and I look back, I think that if I could do it all over again, I would have brought less stuff. Things like an apple peeler and strainer and random things like that. Realistically you rarely eat more than snacks in your room. I realize that I'm glad that I didn't have a roommate, because I need my own space and it would be really hard to share a room with someone the whole time.

On the other hand, the students who had roommates did meet other people more quickly and may not have felt like they were doing it all on their own. I think that the ideal situation is living in a suite where you have separate rooms, but share a common area.

My tip is to talk to other students as much as you can and to keep your door open to encourage people to drop in.

You also really have to put yourself out there and step outside of your comfort zone.

Now that I'm living in a house with other girls, it feels like living in a proper home where students' doors aren't closed and you can sit with people in a common area. I like my own space, but with people around me.

Because it's sometimes hard to find the time or motivation to cook healthy meals, it's easy to eat processed or frozen food or to order in. So, I've even begun ordering from a place that brings specific ingredients for chosen meals to my house once a week, so that all I have to do is to prepare and eat it. It's delicious and healthy and I know I'm eating well. I still have to shop for the basics, such as eggs and milk, but my shopping list is shorter and it doesn't take as long to shop.

Living in residence was just a stepping stone to something much better. Maybe it's being in a home environment and not having to share a washroom or laundry area with so many others. Or being in a program that I actually enjoy, rather than taking a whole bunch of random courses in first year. I have found more people to click with. I am feeling more confident and less anxious. I am so happy that I stuck around, as hard as it was, because if I hadn't, I would never have known that university life could get this good.

ACKNOWLEDGEMENTS

Following my handful of previously conventionally published books, I decided that *Don't Leave, Please Go* would be self-published. I was fortunate enough to be introduced to Doris Chung, at Publisher Production Solutions, to work with me on this. Doris, I couldn't have asked for a more patient and knowledgeable captain on my maiden voyage towards self-publishing. Thank you!

Then, I approached Marney Beck, an editor and longtime friend (who also saw two teens live away from home in university and college) who I met when I first started writing columns for our local newspaper in the late 1980s. No longer a newspaper editor, she now does freelance work and because she has always given me such great advice and tweaked my columns to make them better, I chose her to edit the manuscript. Marney, thanks for your advice and direction. I would never have properly placed the commas, semi colons, periods, brackets, quotation marks and numerals, to name but a few, without you. The many punctuation and grammar rules seem endless, and I am so grateful for your wisdom and expert eyes attending to my work. I think we make a great team!

Don't Leave, Please Go might not have gotten your attention without my oldest daughter, Talia Dimerman, as the fabulous graphic designer behind the cover design. Even though she has been working in the field of graphic design for several years, this is her first attempt at a book cover design, and after many hours and several options (each I thought was perfect until I saw the next!), voila! I had no idea what goes into the design of a book cover—fonts, colour, sizing, a photograph or not, but we have both learned so much along the way and I am even more proud of this book because Talia, you have played such a key role in contributing to its aesthetic appeal.

To my husband, Joey, who has always supported and encouraged me to follow my dreams, I feel so fortunate to have you by my side as a partner and co-parent.

To Chloe, of course I am forever grateful to you for giving me permission to tell our story, because without you going through the highs and lows, sharing them with me (because I know that not every teen does), and staying at university, despite the challenges, there would be no words between this beautifully designed cover. You continue to help me grow as a person and a parent, every day!

Over the years, I have been fortunate to have other experts join me on my *Experts Connect* podcasts. Check them out if you're looking for more information on topics related to what I've written about in *Don't Leave, Please Go*. Such as: tips on how to help your teen transition from high school to university; how to help students develop successful work habits and study for tests and exams; plus a whole lot more. I am thankful to all of these experts and colleagues for helping me help you. Please check out the *Experts Connect* podcast section of my website, helpmesara.com

Also check out my recommended books section to see other books that are great resources, too.

APPENDIX A

List of items to purchase/borrow (choose what works for you)

CLOTHING/FOOTWEAR

- Clothing (for different seasons)
- Underwear/socks
- PJs/nightgown
- Shoes
- Boots & sandals
- Coats/jackets
- Scarf/toque/gloves (if needed)
- Hat

LAUNDRY ITEMS

- Laundry basket (collapsible is best)
- Pop-up hamper
- Laundry detergent
- Anti-static dryer sheets
- Lint roller
- Spot/stain remover stick

SHOWER/HYGIENE/TOILETRIES

- Bath/face towels x 2
- Face washcloths
- Bath robe
- Shower cap

SHOWER/HYGIENE/TOILETRIES CONT'D

- Shampoo & conditioner
- Body wash & sponge
- Shower caddy
- Shaving cream and razors
- Shower shoes (some have holes in them to let the water escape)
- Slippers
- Toothpaste, brush & floss
- Hairbrush/comb/scrunchies
- Hand soap/sanitizer
- Nail scissors/file
- Tweezers
- Medications
- Q-Tips
- Make-up
- Make-up remover
- Hair dryer
- Flat iron straightener
- Feminine hygiene products
- Contact lenses/glass case/ glasses
- Bug spray/sunscreen
- Deodorant

BED ITEMS

- Comforter or duvet & cover
- Blanket or throw
- Decorative pillows
- Pillow or back rest for leaning up against in bed
- Bed riser (if bed is not already high off the ground)
- Sheets (maybe 2 sets)
- Pillow
- Pillow protector
- Pillow cover (2)
- Mattress protector
- Mattress topper (for extra comfort)
- Air mattress & sleeping bag (for guests who stay over)
- Duvet clips (keeps duvet in place inside cover)
- Sheet clips (keeps fitted sheet from coming off mattress)

DECORATIONS/ROOM ACCESSORIES

- Rug (we chose a shaggy white one—big mistake–with all the traffic in and out of the room, it was grey by the end of the school year)
- Tapestry or other wall hanging (makes the room homier)
- Photos or wall hangings
- Step stool (a foldable one)
- Over-bed caddy (in place of bedside table)
- Fan (floor stand is best) & desk fan too if you're inclined to feel warm
- Full-length mirror (over door is best)
- Garbage can
- Boot/shoe tray
- Drape or shower curtain/rod (to conceal clothing closet if no door)
- Erasable board/erasable marker
- Bulletin board & push pins
- Desk lamp & extra lightbulbs
- Closet organizer
- Hangers (for clothes closet)
- Lucite bin stacking drawers/other storage containers
- Sticky tack (in case you want to hang posters, usually no nails allowed)
- Stick-on hooks

SCHOOL/PAPER SUPPLIES

- Stamps (in case they have an urge to send a letter home via snail mail)
- Envelopes/writing paper
- Backpack
- School supplies (e.g. pens, pencils, binders, calendar)
- Paper for printer
- Desk caddy/pen & pencil holder

ELECTRONICS

- Laptop
- Printer
- Router
- Extension cord
- Surge protector
- Head phones

SMALL APPLIANCES/KITCHENWARE/GADGETS

- Small fridge/freezer
- Water filter jug
- Kettle
- Toaster
- Bottle opener
- Utensils
- Mugs
- Plates & bowls
- Water bottle
- Bag/chip clips
- Magnets for fridge
- Cups
- Dish soap and sponge
- Ziploc bags
- Food containers
- Baking soda for fridge
- Thermos
- Can opener
- Small dishrack (the kind that you'd buy for a boat or RV is perfect) or drying mat is good too
- Cutting board and knife
- Banana tree
- Food items (for fridge/ snacks for shelves)

CLEANING SUPPLIES
(MOSTLY FOR USE IN EMERGENCIES OR BY PARENTS WHEN THEY VISIT!)

- Rags
- Stick vacuum/broom & dustpan
- Garbage bags
- Long handled mop & replacement pads/mop head
- Anti-bacterial wipes/liquid cleaner
- Bleach

SAFETY ITEMS

- Batteries
- Flashlight
- Safety kit with band aids etc.

MISCELLANEOUS

- Umbrella
- Measuring tape
- Screwdriver kit
- Sewing kit with needle and thread (as if!)
- Recyclable bags
- Lint Roller
- A permanent marker (to write name or initial on objects) or specialty labels
- Duct tape (to tape drawers shut during moving process)
- Door stopper (door doesn't always stay open without this)

APPENDIX B
MOTHER TO MOTHER (#MTM)

Shortly after my daughter started living in residence, I came across a Facebook post by a mother whose name is Alisa Clamen. She lives in Montreal, (Quebec), Canada. At the time, her son, Jesse Galganov had been missing for a couple of weeks in Peru. Jesse, who was then 22 years old, had been accepted into medical school, and was fulfilling his dream to travel before buckling down to study. Her first-born child, and only son, Alisa describes him as her best friend and soulmate. Back then, she knew, when she hadn't heard from him when he said he would be back in touch, that something was wrong. Ever since that time, Alisa has dedicated the majority of her time to finding Jesse. She has met with government officials (Peru, Canada and the USA, as Jesse is a dual Canadian/American citizen), hired the best search, rescue and recovery team in the world, personally scoured the mountains on which Jesse was last seen and walked in his footsteps herself, and has spent 21 nights sleeping on that mountain.

Like any parent, she has not left any stone unturned. Despite her diligent efforts and unbelievable heartbreak, so far no clue has led to her son's whereabouts. Each day, according to Alisa, is hell. She has learned to put one foot in front of the other, but her life will never be the same until she is hopefully reunited with Jesse. Mom to mom, my heart went out to her and I followed her posts fanatically, hoping for good news. Even though she and I had never met, her desperate attempts to locate her child made me sob and tapped into my worst fears about not being able to locate my children. As she prepared for his departure, she put aside her own desire to have him stay home where she knew he would be safer, in order to honour his desire to pursue his dream. Then, things went horribly wrong.

More recently, Alisa has created a movement called #MTM (mother to mother) because she believes that "only a mother can understand the love that a mother has for her child. To protect them from the world. To make their lives happier than yours. To give them everything. To rescue them when something bad happens." The helplessness that she feels at not being able to get to him—to rescue him—is unfathomable, yet something that we can all connect to.

Alisa is working with Magnus International, a search and recovery company in Israel, to launch a product in Canada and the USA that can help protect you or your loved ones in areas of the world that have limited or no cellular service. She knows that it was not a good idea for Jesse to embark on a solo trip in a less travelled, challenging and unfamiliar terrain and hopes that others travelling—young or more mature—will recognize the importance of being personally prepared, finding safety in numbers and making sure that there are ways to keep in touch with and be located by loved ones. By sharing her message, she is hoping to spare others the heartbreak that she and her family are going through.

And so, I am helping to share her message, too…

For more information, email alisa@alisaclamen.com

ABOUT THE AUTHOR

Sara Dimerman (HelpMeSara) is a psychologist in Ontario, Canada, who has provided counselling to individuals, couples and families for 30 years. She is the author of four other books—two for parents and two for couples.

Prior to *Don't Leave, Please Go*, Sara's most recent book is *Why Married Couples Don't Have Sex…at least not with each other!* (Simon & Schuster, Canada, 2015). She co-authored *How Can I Be Your Lover When I'm Too Busy Being Your Mother* (Simon & Schuster, Canada, 2012). Her second parenting book, *How to Influence your Kids for Good* (Harper Collins, Canada, 2015) was a revised version of *Character is the Key* (Wiley & Sons, Canada, 2009), and her first book, published in 2008 is *Am I A Normal Parent?* (Hatherleigh Press, USA).

Sara's website, helpmesara.com, is regularly updated with new articles and her advice columns, *Experts Connect* podcasts and links to other resources, provides a wealth of information to individuals, parents, couples and families who are looking for help.

Her work also appears in magazines, newspapers and websites around the world; she is a regular guest on radio and television and is often quoted in print.

To be kept up to date on details related to this book, or to purchase a copy, visit dontleavepleasego.com. Connect with her on Facebook: facebook.com/SaraDimermanHelpMeSara or on Twitter @helpmesara.